Praise for
WHY WE SUFFER AND HOW WE HEAL

———

"Dr. Suzan Song has done something remarkable here. Dr. Song's quiet, warm voice carries you along. She transcends typical self-help formulas. This is a really beautiful book."

—**RICK HANSON,** PhD, author of
Buddha's Brain, Hardwiring Happiness, and *Resilient*

"This book is a gift of empathy and lived wisdom—rare, real, and deeply human. Dr. Suzan Song's voice is authentic and courageous; her words speak directly to the heart. Any reader of this book will come away touched, inspired, and grounded in what truly matters."

—**DR. KOEN SEVENANTS,** former global lead for
Mental Health and Psychosocial Support in Emergencies
for UNICEF's Child Protection Area of Responsibility

"In *Why We Suffer and How We Heal,* Dr. Suzan Song brings a message of hope to individuals who feel repeatedly upended by life's adversities. Pain and suffering are ineluctable but traumatization is not. Suffering, when it inevitably comes, points to a path for healing. We can live alongside uncertainty by embracing the instabilities of our daily lives rather than fleeing from them."

—**JAMES L. GRIFFITH,** MD, professor of psychiatry
and behavioral sciences, George Washington University
School of Medicine

"*Why We Suffer and How We Heal* inspires readers to make meaning of life's struggles. Using metaphor and a rich array of case histories, the author draws on her diverse background as an academic, mother, clinician, and explorer in the universal experience of suffering. She is masterful at connecting commonalities among those born into privilege with those subjected to some of the most horrific challenges life has to offer. And the vulnerability she brings when reflecting on her own journey makes her insights exceptionally readable. I particularly appreciate the generous use of 'action tools,' which I've started to incorporate into my own growth. An exceptional contribution to the literature, akin to Frankl's *Man's Search for Meaning;* I will be sharing this widely with colleagues, friends, and family."

—JOSEPH C. KOLARS, MD, MACP, professor of medicine, learning health sciences, and health management and policy, University of Michigan Medical School and University of Michigan School of Public Health

Why We
Suffer
and
How We
Heal

Why We Suffer and How We Heal

Using Narrative, Ritual, and Purpose
to Flourish Through Life's Challenges

Suzan Song, MD, PhD

HARMONY
NEW YORK

Harmony Books
An imprint of Random House
A division of Penguin Random House LLC
1745 Broadway, New York, NY 10019
harmonybooks.com | randomhousebooks.com
penguinrandomhouse.com

Library of Congress Cataloging-in-Publication Data
Names: Song, Suzan J. author
Title: Why we suffer and how we heal / by Suzan J. Song, MD, PhD.
Description: First edition. | New York, NY: Harmony, [2026] |
Includes bibliographical references and index.
Identifiers: LCCN 2025029755 (print) | LCCN 2025029756 (ebook) |
ISBN 9780593581537 hardcover | ISBN 9780593581544 ebook
Subjects: LCSH: Suffering | Adjustment (Psychology) | Healing
Classification: LCC BF789.S8 S667 2026 (print) | LCC BF789.S8 (ebook)
LC record available at https://lccn.loc.gov/2025029755
LC ebook record available at https://lccn.loc.gov/2025029756

Printed in the United States of America on acid-free paper

1st Printing

FIRST EDITION

BOOK TEAM: Production editor: Annette Szlachta • Managing editor:
Allison Fox • Production manager: Meghan O'Leary • Copy editor: Tracy Roe •
Proofreaders: Jane Scarpantoni, Amy J. Schneider, Allison Lindon, Wesley Alspach

Book design by Kevin Quach

The authorized representative in the EU for product safety and compliance
is Penguin Random House Ireland, Morrison Chambers, 32 Nassau Street,
Dublin D02 YH68, Ireland. https://eu-contact.penguin.ie

Dedication

*To my children and mother who keep me
honest, hopeful, and reaching for better,*

To those who ask gently and listen fully,

To those who carry hurt but choose not to wound,

*And to you, the reader, if something in
your life has brought you here.*

PREFACE

You may know people who are seemingly unflappable. Steadfast. Like they've somehow been inoculated with antibodies to render them able to survive, strive, and even thrive through major life stressors and transitions. What is it about these people? Are they born with resilient genes or does culture play a role? Do they have certain outlooks or behaviors that make them able to manage life with grace and confidence, and if so, are these skills everyone can learn?

Despite everyone's deepest wishes, instability visits us all, regardless of income, race, religion, gender, or culture. While some have more severe life stressors than others, all of us will experience an upending of our worlds at some point.

Some people just barrel through it: Just. Keep. Moving. Others may wallow and resign themselves to the situation until they feel motivated to get back into the world again. If this isn't difficult enough, many people tend to believe that they are defective or deficient in some way if they're unable to quickly move on and they search for answers from others. Friends, family, and society often rush in and urge them to see a psychotherapist.

I'm such a therapist. An adult and pediatric psychiatrist, to be precise, for those suffering across the spectrum of despair, from the more common life stressors to the most egregious human rights violations. I've also worked as a humanitarian mental-health adviser, supporting individual-, community-, and systems-level resilience across the globe. In my two decades of clinical care, research, and humanitarian practice, I've been fascinated by those who are successful in being unflappable. Regardless of the complexities in their lives, they are able to handle themselves with self-assurance and poise. I've found that these flourishers have a unique quality: the ability to embrace instability.

We often imagine that stability is what keeps us safe, what spares us from suffering. But in my experience, instability is what invites us into transformation. Some instabilities strike like sudden storms, catastrophic crises that shatter your ability to cope in one single moment. Others creep in slowly, chronic and relentless, wearing you down over time. Some instabilities are clear: the grief of losing a loved one; the disorientation of losing a sense of identity or culture; the ache of ambiguous loss, in which someone is physically gone but psychologically present (or vice versa), as in a breakup or homesickness.

Other instabilities are more nuanced. You may find yourself caught in a stable ambiguity—for instance, stuck in an unhealthy relationship or workplace, unable to move forward yet afraid to leave. Or you might feel a slow erosion of spirit when your values seem misaligned with the world around you, draining your motivation and morale.

Whether born out of your own choices or entirely beyond your control, these instabilities shape your inner landscapes, challenging you to adapt, endure, and grow. But when life tilts you off balance, through loss, change, or rupture, it may not always be the event itself that causes the deepest pain but rather the friction between what the situation is and what you wanted it to be.

The more tightly you grip the illusion of stability, the more disoriented you will be when it slips through your fingers. In relationships, identity, and life, resilience isn't built in the still moments. It's born in the spaces where everything is shifting while you choose to stay grounded.

This book uncovers some of the hidden sources of resilience, confidence, and compassion that I've learned from people across time and space. It provides a framework for how to flourish through instability using time-tested and culturally embraced ways of healing that you can apply regardless of who you are or where you come from. I'd like to share these with you, as I believe these methods work whether you're dealing with major traumas or everyday life challenges.

From my own clinical practice in the United States to my humanitarian work across the globe, I've found universal ways of healing, what I call the "three friends of winter": narrative, rituals, and purpose. These serve as a psychosocial vaccine, to help people embrace the harshness to come.

I was born and raised in the United States, and my psychotherapy training and practice centered on American explanatory models of distress and methods of treatment. I learned to emphasize autonomy, independence, and individuality and was taught that the main path to healing was through an intricate examination and discussion of one's past influences, present inner conflicts, and future goals. Helping people identify and label emotions and draw attention to their thoughts for reflection and manipulation are the mainstays of psychotherapy.

This approach often worked—mostly for highly resourced Americans navigating emotional distress who came to my office in San Francisco, California, and Washington, DC. But I had other patients who came from a variety of backgrounds and cultures and who had spent varying lengths of time in the United States: people who were survivors of torture, children who had been exploited in human trafficking, and families who were displaced due to armed conflict and violence. For many of them, individual talk therapy had limitations—examining their thoughts in an effort to control and master them was not enough. *This can't be it,* I thought, which drove me to uncover other ways of healing.

In addition to being a clinician, I've always had a parallel career as a humanitarian researcher and practitioner, working with former child soldiers in West and East Africa, with displaced Syrian teens in Jordanian refugee camps, and with children in Russian-occupied territories of Ukraine, to name a few. In Burundi, I focused my research on the impact of child soldiering on the next generation: How do parents who are former child soldiers know how to parent if they were in an armed force for the majority of their childhood? What strengths and difficulties are passed down to the next generation? As I was conducting these ethnographic studies, observing, listening, and coding, the clinician in me was drawn to something else: witnessing how people heal.

What I saw was healing not through deep individual introspection but rather through rituals, community gatherings, and a sense of belonging. I brought this back to my clinical work along with another source of healing that I had observed: The power of purpose. A larger perspective.

We can find meaning and self-mastery in hard times through our narratives, but insight alone doesn't always change behavior. Chronic navel-gazing and a mild obsession with yourself can trap you in an insular world of unproductive ruminations, like tumbling through a dryer cycle that never stops.

The general world of psychotherapy looks at the self, and while it's true that narrative can be transformative, that's not always where true healing comes from. We thrive and grow by embedding ourselves in the outside world.

This is where rituals come in. Rituals serve as the bridge between reality and dreams. While narratives clarify values and beliefs, rituals embody them, connecting you to community and culture. Rituals are also important, though, in pointing to something bigger in life: your purpose. Rituals connect you to yourself, your loved ones, and humanity as well as to an energy and presence larger than community.

Narrative, rituals, and purpose—these are the tools that can help all of us adapt during hard times with confidence, assurance, and self-mastery. Instability is challenging, but what makes it unbearable is going through it alone.

I've sat with suffering as an American-trained clinical psychiatrist and an ethnographic researcher. But there's another, more personal lens that influences how I engage with and understand the world: Growing up as a Korean American child, I learned to blend my parents' Korean culture and the dominant American culture around me.

◆ ◆ ◆

Most Korean Americans of my generation grew up with grandparents who survived traumas that rarely made it into history books. The Korean War (1950–1953) was a humanitarian catastrophe that tore families apart and claimed the lives of over three million people, most of them civilians. Entire villages were destroyed; families fled their homes in the dead of the night, crossing frozen rivers and battlefields with children strapped to their backs.

If you know a Korean American family, there's a good chance their history includes stories that were never fully told: grandfathers who were prisoners of war, enduring torture and forced labor; grandmothers who lived in fear of being taken by soldiers as "comfort women"—a euphemism for the systematic sexual slavery imposed by the Japanese military and a trauma that still reverberates in silence. Children were conscripted into militias; civilians were targeted as suspected sympathizers.

These stories—widespread, normalized by war, and often left out of dominant narratives—are carried quietly, unspoken but not unfelt. These invisible histories shaped how families raised their children, how they loved, and how they taught those children to carry pain.

So, as a second-generation Korean American, I've learned to shift between social norms and worldviews, often acting as a bridge between Korean and American communities. An emotional fluency of sorts lets me know when to bow or shake hands or when silence speaks louder than words. Bicultural kids learn to observe closely and listen carefully, attuned to what's *not* being said, understanding what it's like to be the one who doesn't quite fit in.

Reorienting, recalibrating, and adapting over and over in new cities, learning different rules, and immersing oneself in vastly different cultures builds skills in pivoting, staying grounded in instability, and developing a strong internal compass that holds complexity with confidence.

While my formal training is in Western psychiatry, in my global mental-health research and humanitarian practice, I developed a cultural understanding of pain that isn't always linear or logical. But my way of seeing suffering has been shaped just as much by family stories as by any textbook.

Throughout my clinical and humanitarian practice, I've had to determine which human instincts and actions can help us thrive in all seasons, including the winters of life. In Asian art, the *three friends of winter* refers to a motif of pine, bamboo, and plum blossoms—plants that thrive in even the harshest of winters. Paintings of the trio covered the walls of my childhood home, representing the skill of living with hope and perseverance in the face of adversity. These three-friends-of-winter tools have shaped how I work and changed how I live. My hope is that as we move forward, they'll do the same for you.

CONTENTS

INTRODUCTION

"At age fifteen, I was more comfortable with an AK-47 or machete than with a pencil," Charles remembers as he shifts on a three-legged stool in his concrete home in Bujumbura, Burundi. Child soldiering for eight years is hard on the body; he can't sit for long periods, so we move our interview to the forest to walk and talk in privacy. I am prepared to hear the stories of escaping life-threatening mobs and isolation. I am not expecting to experience it myself.

Before beginning my PhD work in Burundi, I had studied multiple worlds of healing throughout my medical training, residency, and fellowship. While my master's degree in public health policy gave conceptual models, it was Zulu healers in South Africa who showed me that knowledge lives in relationships. In post-earthquake Haiti, I saw the strength with which people managed to rebuild.

Through it all, I was struck by the resilience of those who had lost everything. Amid ruins and grief, people somehow pushed through the devastation and quietly rebuilt. It wasn't just endurance—there was something about the human capacity to reimagine, carry hope, and find calm. I wanted to understand how, after the ground shifts and the world fractures, people still find a way not just to stand but to feel alive.

It doesn't take a scientist to know that being a child soldier leaves deep scars—depression, anxiety, the weight of trauma that lingers long after the war ends. But I wanted to understand more than just the aftermath. I wanted to see how those whose childhoods had been stolen—some taken as young as ten—made sense of their own histories.

In Sierra Leone and Liberia, I met men and women who as children had been forced to fight, steal, and survive in ways no child should. Many struggled with disconnected relationships, restless nights, and memories that wouldn't let go. Most people turn off the radio or TV when they hear stories of extreme trauma—they don't know what to do with the helplessness, and the pain is too close to bear, so they turn away.

I did the opposite. I wanted to hear the stories—not through the lens of pathology but through the survivors' own words. So I pursued a PhD at the University of Amsterdam and used an ethnographic approach to study intergenerational stress among former child soldiers in Burundi. What does survival look like, not just in the moment but across time and generations? I wanted to understand their past as well as the future they were shaping.

Known for its coffee plantations and lounging hippos by the beach, Burundi is the size of Maryland, bordered by Rwanda and the Democratic Republic of the Congo. In 1993, the assassination of the country's first democratically elected Hutu president triggered a civil war, a brutal conflict between Hutus and Tutsis. Intensified by the spillover from neighboring Rwanda's genocide, the war claimed the lives of over three hundred thousand people and displaced more than one million. Though a formal peace treaty was signed in 2001, many small factions simmered. Lasting over a decade, the war continued on with the help of a secret weapon: children.

Around the world, there are an estimated 250,000 children conscripted into the armed forces. While many envision a child soldier as a drugged boy with red eyes slinging an AK-47 over his shoulder, 40 percent of child soldiers are unarmed girls and boys. In addition to working as fighters, these children are used as porters, sex slaves, messengers, and cooks. Why are so many children exploited into soldiering?

In countries with predominantly young populations, armed groups have a steady supply of potential soldiers. Children, still in the early stages of cognitive and moral development, often struggle to grasp the full weight of their actions. Highly impressionable, they are vulnerable to coercion and are often manipulated through fear, false promises, or forced drug use. Their neuroplasticity makes them fast learners, easy to train for the most dangerous assignments. Teens are idealistic with a strong sense of social justice—when an uncle or parent is murdered, revenge pulls them into an armed group; it's similar to the social calling of gangs around the world.

This was the case for Charles. At ten years old, he fled his village with his parents and uncle after Burundi's first elected president was killed. "I stayed with strangers, sometimes passing the night in banana trees with nowhere else to go," he tells me as his eyes gaze past his toddler, who is waddling over sticks beneath her feet.

With the end of war, these former child soldiers were expected to be civilians. Now they were having children of their own. How did they fare as parents? What strengths and struggles, if any, were passed on to the next generation? Did they ever find stability? These were questions I had come across the globe to study, not only for what the answers might tell us about these woeful legacies of war but also for what they might tell us about how all people—those who have experienced the worst humanity has to offer as well as those who suffer more "everyday" hurts—can reclaim their lives.

❖   ❖   ❖

I spend the day with Charles and his family, observing their daily life. The scar on his forehead is a silent testament to what he has endured. At ten, he survived in the jungle, wielding a machete for food, forced into combat under the influence of amphetamines and cocaine. He hadn't signed up for war; he had been promised safety and a stable job. Instead, he found himself trapped.

But it wasn't the violence of war that nearly broke him—it was returning home. During the conflict, he had been ordered to attack his own village. When the war ended, his community did not forgive or forget. Branded a monster, he was met with rejection. His neighbors warned their children to stay away, later calling his son a killer's son. For Charles, the battlefield had changed, but the war continued.

The day is ending, so my interpreter, Emmanuel, rushes me off, as he does every day, to avoid threat. "It's time, Dr. Suzan," Emmanuel whispers. "Night is coming quickly. We must leave now."

I stumble off the stool and wince as gravel fills my sandals and pierces the soles of my uncallused feet. Charles comes to my side, smiling in a gentlemanly, hospitable manner, and leads me out of the house.

As I moved toward the car, Charles leans in and whispers, hot breath condensing on my earlobe, "You should be careful." He's so close I can almost feel his pulse pounding, as mine now is. "People here do not live in a good way with neighbors even. One day they are laughing with you, inviting you to their house, their kitchen, for dinner. Then they will kill you at night. They will kill for a SIM card."

His words are in Kirundi and incomprehensible to me, but Emmanuel later fills me in on what I had sensed—Charles's dirty hands on my arms and the intensity of his stare suggest sexual innuendo. Within what seems like seconds, a dozen young men, some with AK-47s slung across their shoulders, join Charles and descend upon our truck, encircling me and blocking my view as I try to search for my team.

In one minute, Emmanuel is shoving our team into the truck, and the next minute, I'm inhaling dust as we book it out of the commune. Out of the corner of my eye, I catch the men smirking and retreating. Emmanuel spends the next hour on the phone. I didn't quite understand what Charles told me, but it's clear that Emmanuel is deeply alarmed.

At last we approach a secluded lot. Emmanuel, a man of few

words, parks the car and turns to look me in the eye. Emmanuel is clear: "They are after you. It is not safe here. Stay in the house. Those ex-coms"—ex-combatant former child soldiers—"want to kill you," he warns.

His words are not registering. I want to grab him and tell him he is mistaken; the trusting American in me cannot believe someone would turn on me so quickly. I tell him that, but my naive dismissal of his fears is met with pleas to take the danger seriously. Emmanuel urges me to call my local Burundian friend so he can convince me to leave the country. Together, they work out a plan to hide me in a room across town.

As night falls, I lie awake, unable to comprehend the gravity of the situation. I ask myself: *How did I, a single Korean American woman, end up alone in a remote village hiding from former child soldiers who want my cash? Why, exactly, am I here?*

Trying to Die

It wasn't an accident that I ended up alone, targeted for murder, thousands of miles away from loved ones. While altruism and intellectual curiosity were factors in my decision to work with children who had experienced anguish, I must admit that my real motivation seemed personal. I couldn't quite understand it, but it felt like a compulsion—it felt as if I were trying to heal. I just wasn't sure from what.

My path to becoming a physician was never just about saving lives. It was about understanding suffering—the kind that lingers in the body and mind long after the wounds have closed. At the University of Michigan, I created my own major, epistemology across cultures, drawn to the ways different societies made sense of pain and healing. I set my course after a chance encounter with a Bangladeshi woman whose face had been forever changed by an acid attack after she refused a man's advances. I decided I would become a burn surgeon for girls and women like her.

But in medical school, while my peers thrived on the precision of anatomy, I found myself more captivated by the uncertainty within the human experience. Surgery, I realized, was not my calling. Psychiatry, however, quietly chose me.

While my training at the University of Chicago, Harvard, and Stanford opened exceptional doors, I discovered my deepest learning happened beyond these privileged spaces—in emergency departments (EDs), where I met the extremes of human despair: patients who swallowed paper clips, attempted suicide with chain saws, or returned to the ED again and again, teetering on the edge. It was never the act of self-destruction alone that interested me; it was the stories of childhood wounds that had never properly healed, the systematic neglect that prevented resilience, and the profound human need to be seen that was never met.

In my practice today, I move between worlds, from supporting high-profile CEOs and political figures managing unprecedented stress to working with children who are seeking asylum or escaping human trafficking. What connects these seemingly different populations is surprisingly universal: our shared vulnerability and capacity for both suffering and healing.

In chasing suffering, I was also testing my own limits, walking a fine line between bearing witness and being consumed. I thought I was simply trying to understand, but some might say I was trying to get myself killed. Maybe I was. While hiding from former child soldiers in Burundi, I asked myself, *How did I get here?*

That's when a bolt of insight knocked me upside the head: *Ah,* I thought. *It's about Dad.*

Dad

On February 15, 1993, at two in the morning, my mother greeted unexpected visitors at our front door: a pair of police officers. Earlier that evening, after my father had routinely closed our liquor store and headed to the van with the day's earnings, he was approached by two men. They decided to steal not just the money but also the van and not just to threaten but to outright assault him.

My father's defensive punches were met with knives. Then he was shoved into the van. Believing they had killed him, the assailants blathered on about where to drop his body. Instead of playing dead, my father lunged for the panel door, opened it, and threw himself out of the moving van. He crawled half a mile, with 80 percent of his lungs collapsed and stab wounds to both kidneys, able only to whisper for help. A motel clerk noticed him bleeding on the side of the road and called 911.

Later that morning, I awoke to my mother sitting next to me on my twin bed. She rested her hands on my arm and said, "*Aigoo.* Your dad is in the hospital. There was a robbery. We need to visit today." Like a mail carrier, she dropped the news, then left.

My first thought was *Do I need to cancel my piano lesson?* This wasn't the first robbery, and I wasn't yet aware it would be the last. I was fifteen years old at the time, making soap in science class and practicing lacrosse throws. Life was fairly simple in my eyes: My mother worked three jobs, and my father worked six days a week at the liquor store, leaving me an experienced latchkey kid. I got myself home from school every day, microwaved Dinty Moore beef stew, and watched reruns of *Family Ties* and *Oprah* as background noise while I did my homework.

My father struggled for his life in the shock trauma unit, and even so, I kept my GPA at a solid 3.7. Three times a week, my mother would leave work early and drive me to the hospital, visits that replaced piano lessons and lacrosse practice. The tubes snaking into my father's nose and the knife wounds across his jaundiced skin didn't scare me as much as the change in his eyes. He was a different person. The dad who sang "Calendar Girls" while driving me to camp was no longer there.

Eventually, a deep quiet seeped into my soul. I continued to be on time for school, made dinner, and loaded the laundry. If anyone asked how I was doing or why I had to miss lacrosse practice, I responded matter-of-factly, without emotion: "All is fine, just studying and stuff."

Psychiatrists call this *isolation of affect*, a psychological defense mechanism to avoid pain. I didn't miss a beat at school, and yet, numbed to the world, I was slowly slipping into a gaping hole. As my father was dying, I was figuring out how to live a newly uncertain and unstable life, with no road map to follow. I longed more and more for a stuffed animal, a friend—anyone—to absorb me and all my fears, helplessness, and loneliness.

Stability became my lifeline, and I cemented it with working—at school, at home, at my ice cream parlor job. Soon it became clear that my only comfort in life came through productivity. Doing something became a surrogate for a warm shower or cuddles with my dog. Staying busy filled the gaps between thinking about my father languishing alone in the hospital and confronting a primal fear that lived in my core.

My father died in his hospice bed on March 6, 1994. While his death didn't take away the few memories I had of him, his loss prevented the possibility of future memories. His death was my first major loss, and I spent the hours and probably days immediately following it in shock. Sharp memories punctuate the dull ones: the hearse making its way through the neighborhood game of sharks and minnows; the clear nail polish that was supposed to prevent a run from expanding on my black funeral stockings.

For years, I didn't feel the need to talk about losing my dad. I was fully aware of it, but I stayed silent. I didn't create a narrative about his death or his life. He made guest appearances in my dreams, though, as a pedestrian crossing the street. I held him close through every life struggle: a breakup, my mother's breast cancer, the loss of my dog. I held conversations with him in my mind, but otherwise, I largely ignored the impact of his loss.

Slowly, those imagined conversations occupied less and less of my time. While I was grieving the loss of my father, his death was also the beginning of the end of a relationship with myself. Without context or words to wrap around what had happened, I pressed forward, desperate for stability and trying to move on.

After-school jobs replaced loitering at the mall; long study days prevented drinking with college friends; and the treadmill of advanced education postponed dating, financial planning, having kids, taking risks, and learning from mistakes. This was the opportunity cost of chasing stability: isolation, struggle, and emotional exhaustion with the constant buzz of tumult. My lens was singularly focused on the future—"when things settle down."

That was because the present felt saturated with unease. *Push aside and numb the pain to just get through it. Head down, work hard.* I had a sense that this wasn't the ideal way to cope, but I didn't know any other strategy. I wanted to slow down, feel, and engage with the world differently. But I didn't know how. Unbeknownst to me, the fight for stability and my desire to press on after my father's death influenced my choices in work and love.

Your house, your car, even your loved ones can be taken away from you, I reasoned, but no one can take your education. Financial security became a prerequisite for personal safety. Consequently, I took what felt like the most assured path to stability: I became a physician, which led to my work in psychiatry and public health. Despite my conscious pursuit of stability in my career, something deeper drove me to subvert that stability and find danger.

I was hiding in Burundi when I came to a sudden realization: I had put my life at risk because I still held my father's shocking death in silence. Without the words to understand what had happened, I was doomed to relive it continuously—and now vicariously, with my own life-threatening experience. I had been studying trauma and resilience without realizing I was seeking to understand—and heal—myself.

Have You Experienced Instability?

We all have so much in common. Some people have harrowing stories of torture, child trafficking, or being held hostage, and others have the more familiar stories of broken relationships, unexpected losses, and public failures, but extraordinary upheaval and more ordinary pain share common themes. Regardless of the cause of suffering, everyone deserves to feel empowered and be equipped to heal.

Perhaps you have had a relationship with someone who was demeaning, hypercritical, and controlling, or maybe you saw someone assault a loved one. Maybe you were bullied as a child, have chronic pain or an intractable mental-health condition, or grew up in relative poverty. These adversities can cause significant lifelong hardships and a sense of aloneness.

So, whatever your background, this book is for you. It will guide you through the three pillars of healing that I've developed through my work across cultures and contexts. The wide range of dangers and uncertainties in our daily lives can flatten us, sink us deeper and deeper into despair and avoidance. We minimize our suffering because we feel we should be able to manage better. Lost and confused each time our lives are upended, we reflexively crave a former era of perceived stability.

This makes sense, as humans are hardwired to pursue stability. According to evolutionary psychology, the human psyche has been shaped by threats from the natural world since the Stone Age. Shelter, food, and clothing were limited and unpredictable. At the mercy of wild predators, our ancestors were desperate for stability. Their competitive advantage? Psychological strength. Those who survived likely tried to avoid loss and uncertainty—when life hangs by a thread, even the smallest tug can bring it all down. Those who pulled through did so because they had the ability to attain security and reproduce.

In one of the most sophisticated experiments conducted on the relationship between uncertainty and stress, Archy de Berker at University College London had forty-five volunteers play a video game that involved turning over rocks that might be hiding snakes beneath them. When participants uncovered a snake, they got zapped on the hand.

Researchers then had subjects guess whether or not a rock hid a snake before the rock was turned over. The volunteers learned which rocks likely hid snakes, but the researchers then changed the parameters, increasing the volunteers' uncertainty of whether or not a snake would be present. Participants' stress levels were measured by self-reporting and by physiological markers of stress, such as pupil dilation and perspiration. The researchers found that when volunteers had high uncertainty about whether a shock was coming, they were more stressed than when they were certain they'd get a shock. In other words, people would rather know for sure that they're about to be laid off or dumped than deal with uncertainty.

Stability Is an Illusion

In my work, I began to observe and listen to those who seemed to flourish in the face of life's afflictions and was stunned by the commonality I found among those who thrived: Their ability to build inner peace was less about the extent of horrors they'd suffered and more about giving up the illusion of stability. They embraced and engaged with instability and thereby carried themselves with a certain level of fortitude and calm.

In the thick of crises, people often feel instability is a fatal blow from which there is no return. Many explain their suffering to me through a personal assessment—typically narratives that try to end their despair but seem to perpetuate it. I can't count the number of times people have come into my office and said they'd never find love and would be single for life. Their self-diagnosis was ultimately that they just couldn't manage the instability of dating, depriving themselves of confidence and purpose. To me, this is a tragedy. We need purpose and a sense of self-efficacy to manage the disruptions that are sure to arrive.

Once the storm has passed, we want to press forward. Relieved to finally be in the clear and bewildered that we made it through, we can't imagine any benefit to looking back. We want to move on and put the past behind us. But when you move forward without processing the upheaval, you miss the opportunity to learn about your natural strength. And becoming aware of your natural strengths is what can gird you for the next inevitable disruption.

The Three Friends of Winter

After visiting my father in the hospital, I would sit for hours flipping through old family photos in our living room, my haven through that dark winter. Covering the walls were my father's Buddhist scrolls—Korean paintings of protective tigers and masks, as well as motifs of the three friends of winter—pine, bamboo, and plum blossoms—plants that thrive even in the harshest of winters.

As I listened to the stories of people across the spectrum of despair, I began to notice that there are common elements that can sink or float people. It became clear to me that the three friends of winter—the tools that allow us to weather the toughest blustering storms—are narrative, rituals, and purpose.

My goal is for you to gain a deeper curiosity and understanding of how you engage in the world. That understanding will allow you to find more agency and confidence during the inevitable ups and downs. Make no mistake, though, understanding yourself more fully will not generate constant happiness—that is not my goal for you. To me, living a full life means having a wide range of emotions and experiences and finding comfort that going through difficulties will not collapse you—it will enrich you.

This book is about being alive and finding peace. It's also about suffering. My most important aim in this book is to explore the relationship between the two: why we suffer and how we heal.

Part 1 of this book, "Narrative," describes the role that stories and explanations play in people's lives, exploring the hidden backstories that are the main drivers of how they perceive and react to realities. Part 2, "Rituals," helps put intentions and beliefs into practice. In this section, we'll see how rituals are used to honor those we have lost, let go of a desperate clinging to a need for certainty through examples of ambiguous loss, and undergo a process of self-transformation as we integrate our past selves into the present.

Part 3, "Purpose," builds on these elements of the self and wishes for a different type of reality to engage with a larger sense of connection and meaning in the world. Living a meaningful life means engaging with the instabilities at hand and allowing a sense of calmness and resonance. You'll learn what it means to be grounded, to live a life of coherence that aligns with your desired narratives and rituals. You'll learn how you might have, unknowingly, defined a purpose in order to fulfill an unmet need, and you'll learn how your narratives and rituals can be used to fuel a life purpose.

I call these tools the three friends to emphasize the importance of interconnectedness. We all know that relationships matter. In the West, especially in America, most of us have absorbed the message that strong social ties are good for your health, just like sleep, a healthy diet, and exercise. We've slotted *connection* onto the wellness checklist—schedule time with friends, attend a community event, maybe call a parent or adult child once a week. But underneath this tidy framework is a transactional view of relationships in which people become resources, and connection becomes a means to an end. We value independence so deeply that dependence can feel like weakness and needing others can feel like failure.

But in many relationally interdependent cultures around the world, the self doesn't float alone. Identity is shaped *with* others, not *next to* them. To belong is not a goal; it's a given. In these societies, your existence is inseparable from the roles you play in the lives of others: daughter, neighbor, friend, witness, caregiver. Dependency isn't shameful; it's simply part of the human experience. And it's through those mutual ties—sometimes burdensome, sometimes beautiful—that people find resilience, meaning, and healing.

In the United States, we're living through a loneliness epidemic, yet people often try to fix loneliness with the same tools that created it—with more self-optimization, more curated connections, more autonomy. My goal is not to help you be better at doing life alone but to remind you that you were never meant to do life alone in the first place.

This book is based on true stories of my patients, my research participants, and those I have worked with in humanitarian practice as well as leaders shaping change at the systems level. To protect their privacy, names and details have been changed. In many cases, I have used composite characters to represent an amalgam of more than one person, but the core of their stories remains intact. While a small portion of these accounts addresses violence and violation, most explore moments of courage, connection, and everyday life. These pages are here for you to explore in your own time and in the way that feels most right for you.

Some of the stories are shocking and others are more familiar, but all are versions of what everyone is capable of dealing with. Each story reveals common elements of suffering, offers insights into the human condition, and provides lessons you can carry forward as you navigate your own challenges.

I want to be clear that I do not believe that the more common painful situations I describe—breakups, work conflicts, and family stress—are equivalent to enduring torture, trafficking, kidnapping, genocide, and child soldiering. Torture and human rights violations fracture any analogy. However, these stories all show how the three friends of winter can be used to shape and ease suffering across the spectrum.

Understanding how we managed past struggles informs us of our natural ways of coping. Too often, people are unaware of how stressful experiences affect their lives. Behaviors and habits get written off as personality issues. People are generally not sure why they feel and behave in problematic ways, so they don't understand that they have choices in how they respond.

This should bring all of us some relief: You can choose to appreciate what instability teaches you. Because everyone often experiences conflict and hardship, you can learn to more fully respect and appreciate moments of calm. Your setbacks can teach you how to feel and express compassion. When you uncover the hidden patterns and forces that shape both the creation of chaos and your response to instability, you become unflappable, able to live with more inner peace and control, regardless of your struggle.

PART I

NARRATIVE

Pine (소나무, *sonamu*, in Korean; 松樹, *sōngshù*, in Chinese, 松, *matsu*, in Japanese): Evergreen in nature, tall, and with deep roots, pine represents fortitude with a strong foundation, moral uprightness, and an ability to withstand harsh winter conditions for centuries. In Asian art, pine symbolizes steadfastness, perseverance, and resilience.

Losing a parent during my childhood did a strange thing to me. In the years after my father's death, I cropped out normal adolescent stuff and focused on the reality of being a grown-up. Burying my childhood so I could function as an adult, I fixated on work. I wanted the security of knowing I had a stash of money in case of emergencies. The logic went something like this: *If we'd had more money, we wouldn't have needed to own a liquor store. If we hadn't owned a liquor store, my father wouldn't have been assaulted. If he hadn't been assaulted, he would still be alive and with me today.* My conclusion, therefore: Having money means personal safety.

With this in mind, I quickly picked up a few jobs: scooping ice cream, answering phones at a real estate agent's office, and, the most lucrative job of all, waiting tables at a Bennigan's restaurant. It turned out that anticipating customers' needs and serving them was something I was good at. Carrying two to three dishes stacked on my forearms while gliding between staff and patrons as if I were on roller skates kept me challenged throughout the night. In a system based on tips, I was conscious of being friendly, accommodating, and nonintrusive.

A seemingly ordinary couple came in for dinner and ordered a Monte Cristo sandwich to share. *Won't make much off of this table,* I thought.

But the woman was cordial and clearly wanted to engage me in conversation. In a subtle Maryland accent, she asked, "Are you still in school, hon?"

I told her I was indeed in high school. "What are you doin' this job for?" she asked, and followed that with a barrage of questions about what I wanted to study in college and, of course, the common question among new people I met: "Where are you from?"

I told her I was working a few jobs to save up for college and hoped to go to medical school and that my family was from Korea, aware that that was what most people were actually asking.

"Wow. Y'all made it all the way over here?"

I was confused, as I had been born and raised in Maryland, but before I could clarify this point for her, she leaned toward me, put her hand on my arm, and said, clearly emotionally enthralled, "That is just so amazin', hon, that you escaped the North Korea for a better life."

Now, I like to think of myself as a fairly honest person. After getting caught lying to my parents at nine years old—I'd told them my brother drew on the living-room table when in fact I was the culprit—I challenged myself never to lie again. That childhood experiment probably accounts for why I'm a horrible poker player—my emotions are fairly transparent.

"Oh, my family is from South Korea and I was born and raised here in Maryl—" I started.

She interrupted, her eyes now glassy with impending sympathy tears: "You are so strong, child. It is honorable that you're helping your family to safety."

There are times when I want to clarify and explain myself in the hopes of changing someone's perception of me. This was not one of them. With a smile, I dashed off to attend to other customers. When I sensed the single-sandwich couple was ready to leave, I placed the folder with the twenty-five-dollar check on their table, said, "Enjoy the rest of your night," and left to take care of other customers, as the crowd was picking up. Later, when I passed by their now empty table, I noticed the corner of something white sticking out of the check holder. Inside was a business card with a woman's name and the address of a hair studio on the front. On the back was an encouraging message: *Go pursue your dreams!* To my surprise, behind the card lay a hundred-dollar tip.

While the story about me being a North Korean defector wasn't true, the tale shows something profound about humans: our desire for stories.

Blueprints of Internal Dialogue

Narratives about who we are, who we were, and why things are happening around us permeate every moment of our lives. We are each essentially a collection of stories and explanations—those that we tell and those that we are told. While we don't have control over the stories that are told about us, we do have control over those that we tell.

The internal dialogue of your narrative helps you understand what you've experienced and who you were, are, and want to be going forward. My teenage-formed belief that my father would still have been alive if we'd had more financial security was a narrative that had a profound impact on the personal and career decisions I made in adulthood.

We construct blueprints of narratives that define how we experience the world—the narratives explain what happens to us but also alter our perceptions of experiences and even our reality. Shaping the logic of our stories, this inner dialogue controls how you explain your life, your beliefs about how the world works, how you should conduct yourself, and who you are. Narratives give a play-by-play guide for how to move through the world. Crafting reality to match experiences, narratives are an emotional grammar that gives structure to how we need to feel.

The problem is, most people are relatively unaware of their narratives or use them to stay bound in something known and familiar, protective but agonizing. Many people believe that the ability to get through hard times depends on the ability to barrel through it, sometimes creating extra tasks to avoid facing problems and putting the past behind them as quickly as possible. Others ruminate on the same explanations of how they were wronged and constantly analyze actions around them.

Suffering is due not only to the actual event but to the narratives around the experience. While we reflexively want to avoid suffering, the best method for getting through hard times may not be barreling through. Rather, those who have found relative calm during chaos engage in a process that we can all learn: rewriting narratives.

1

Story of Stories

Wearing only socks, Maya ran out her front door. A baby was snuggled in a car seat that hung from the crook of her left elbow. Yelling with desperation that filled the front yard, Maya rocked the car seat back and forth and gestured wildly to emphasize her anguish. The thirty-six-year-old former corporate lawyer wasn't signaling for help for a medical emergency—it was a mothering one. She had reached her limits as a parent.

This is what brings her to my office a week later. Isolated from friends and family, Maya is sleep-deprived and relentlessly on call—her anger is justified. Understimulated and overtasked, she believes she is failing as a mother if she outsources any of her responsibilities.

Like a light switch, she has only two modes: over-functioning and doing the job of two or three, and underfunctioning by emotionally numbing herself in streaming shows after the kids fall asleep. Without conscious awareness, she is trying to make her husband happy by validating his needs while keeping her own hidden.

Week after week, Maya holds on to stories of disappearance and overwhelm with the same cast of characters and plot to explain and validate her suffering. Struggling with growing resentment, she feels wholly dissatisfied with her life. As she dreams about divorce or potential movie-like romances, she finds herself in perpetual instability. She sinks lower and lower into a dark abyss. Unclear how she got here, she struggles to find a way out of the discontentment of motherhood and the family that she thought she wanted.

Maya sees irritability and crawling-out-of-her skin frustration as a symptom of something larger: She believes she isn't as good a mother as others are. Thinking that not breastfeeding her child is worse than death and disease and wildfires, she tends her cracked, bleeding nipples to infection. Maya is like many of the new mothers whom I see in my clinical practice—loving, competent women who are taken aback when the support they expected doesn't arrive. She's now integrated her presumed failure at motherhood into her self-concept and identity.

Without a career to focus on, she defines herself as lazy and insignificant. She thinks, *I should be able to do this. I shouldn't need a break. I don't deserve to have time to myself.* Fear of making a mistake replaces the confidence she took for granted at work. Consumed by the fear that she will fail her children in some way, Maya is agitated and chronically unsettled.

I remember this blur, the nights speckled with nursing, then managing the scary dreams my kids had as their imaginations developed. I searched for breast-milk catchers and under-eye creams to survive the day, stumbled, and repeated it all the next day.

Over the past decade, I've worked with a growing number of patients like Maya, people who appear to have the full range of privileges—excellent schooling, nurturing home environments, financial cushioning, and robust health—yet still struggle with the instabilities that come with major life transitions. Not only are they stunned and confused on how to move forward; they're having meltdowns in the front yard.

Maya joined the cadre of my patients, my friends, and myself who were all in similar situations, but she had a strikingly different response. She focused sharply on her ensnarement in a cultural trap: the martyrdom of motherhood.

Despite their best efforts, many people around the world fall into accepting society's expectations of parenting. Behind the tears of frustration and isolation are decades upon decades of stories about how mothers should be. Desperate to hide from society's gaze, many mothers render themselves invisible after ineffective protest. Motherhood and marriage are, at the most basic level, acts of perseverance.

And yet some mothers manage to stay grounded amid the chaos of new parenthood. What stands out isn't their willingness to embrace the myth of the self-sacrificing mother—it's their courage to question it. These are women who redefine what motherhood means on their own terms, letting go of inherited expectations and choosing to follow what's truly best for themselves and their children—and absolving themselves of any guilt.

Whether it's the self-sacrificial mothers, the altruistic health-care workers who believe they should always put patients before themselves, or the always-on professionals who think they should constantly be busy, people absorb cultural scripts that may run deeper than intellect.

Psychologists have long understood that the way people frame their experiences—what they tell themselves about what's happening—shapes how they feel and what they do next. As Viktor Frankl, an Austrian neurologist, psychiatrist, and Holocaust survivor, famously wrote, "When we are no longer able to change a situation, we are challenged to change ourselves."

Yet change doesn't necessarily mean working harder or thinking more positively; it may mean updating the story you think you're living.

The goal isn't to completely disavow or reject your social narratives. It's to recognize that we're all shaped by narratives—both personal and cultural—that we didn't consciously choose. And often, our narratives are driven by emotions we haven't yet named, let alone understood.

The Actor Who Never Auditioned

Maya feels a deep sense of inner instability despite everything in her life appearing stable, an experience that psychologists are beginning to understand more deeply. Termed *cognitive entrapment through identity scripts,* these are inherited, often implicit expectations people absorb about how they're supposed to behave in a given role—especially when that role is closely tied to an identity, like mother, leader, or provider. The problem is, people often aren't even aware of these scripts.

It's like you've been cast in a play you never auditioned for and maybe never wanted to be in; as if you're handed a script, a costume, and pushed onto a stage. At first, you know you're acting and you try your best, but over time, you forget it's an act. The character's lines start to feel like your own voice. Eventually, you stop questioning the role, since it feels like the only way to be, the only recognizable version of yourself. A script tells you how a good mother or loyal partner should act, and it provides structure and offers predictability, which feels like stability.

Yet most of the time, these scripts do the opposite. The more tightly you hold on to these stories about who you are, the more likely you are to get stuck—reacting the same way over and over, even when better options are right in front of you. Sometimes you hold on to interpretations or thoughts that hurt you simply because they fit the story you've always told yourself. They're familiar, and familiarity feels safe.

Promising certainty, these identity schemas can often suppress growth. You might stay in a role you've outgrown, tolerate dynamics that don't serve you, or ignore discomfort out of the belief that this is just how it's supposed to be. Even when you know what needs to be done, making it happen is a whole different challenge.

◆   ◆   ◆

Early in her career, Herminia Ibarra, now a professor at London Business School, was intrigued by a pattern she kept seeing in high-potential professionals. These people didn't lack competence—they were smart, capable, and driven. But when they were promoted into leadership roles, many of them faltered. Not because they couldn't do the job but because they couldn't *see themselves* in the role.

Ibarra decided to study how people became leaders—not only

through skill, but through identity. In a now-classic study, she followed professionals in consulting and banking as they moved into management roles. What she found was striking: People struggled most not with tasks or strategy but with the inner conflict between their old identity scripts and the new expectations of leadership.

Technical experts often build their reputation and identity on being detail-oriented and able to solve problems quickly. But if they're promoted to management, the necessary skills often shift to delegation, vision-setting, and personnel management. These people may know what the role requires, but emotionally, they struggle to let go of the story that their worth comes from their technical expertise. So even though an organization may say you are ready for leadership, internal schemas shaped by culture, reward systems, and professional norms can create a psychological tension between past success and future potential.

Ibarra found that the most successful leaders weren't those who forced themselves into the new molds but those who experimented with new narratives, trying on different ways of being, adapting the script over time until it fit both their new roles and their authentic selves. Sometimes the biggest barrier to growth isn't a lack of skill. It's the silent loyalty you feel to the definition of an identity you might not have chosen but have been living for years.

From the moment people are born, they're told what school to attend, what jobs they should attain, what partners they should marry, even how much they should weigh and what they should wear. The stories they tell themselves don't just describe reality; they actively construct it. In order to adequately address the influence of social narratives on your way of being, you need to spotlight your personal narratives. After all, developing stories and explanations about our experiences is part of how we evolve as humans.

"First We Invented Stories, Then They Changed Us"

Before humans had language, they had what psychology professor Merlin Donald called the "mimetic mind"—they used pointing, gesturing, vocalizations, and facial expressions to communicate with one another, conveying the essence of the past and a crude future plan. A hunter could wade along the bank of a river with his friend, then point and grunt at the school of fish he intended to nab. Women could demonstrate tools such as grinding stones to prepare food.

The advent of verbal language allowed more precision and efficiency in expressing thoughts and feelings; now people could communicate what they expected of others, define what was emotionally engaging, and validate others' feelings. With verbal language, they could construct an explanation of why someone did something, taking into account personality, situation, history, beliefs, and desires. Our forebears could keep track of what others had done and were doing, reinforce and broadcast social norms, and state risks and options. This use of narrative took off with the help of two critical elements: overwhelmed mothers and fire.

Around 1.6 million years ago, life was challenging. I assume parenting was a nightmare, given that mothers had to keep infants safe from saber-toothed tigers and harsh winters. Children required more care than a single person could provide, hence the development of alloparenting. Infants and young children were cared for by female kin, allowing mothers to have more children and sooner, and caretakers used narratives to share stories and explanations about the children.

Around the same time, fire-making and thus cooking became more routine, leading to both social and physical evolution. When the sun went down and the temperatures dropped, people could now huddle around a fire. Under the moon and stars, alert to a distant howl or a quiet snap of a twig, they could find comfort in one another. They shared stories to pass the time, entertain, and build a sense of shared values.

Fire also contributed to physical changes. Cooking with heat broke food down and made it more digestible, so humans no longer needed such large mandibular (jaw) muscles. Natural selection led to smaller jaws, which allowed space for the cranium to house a larger brain—a brain that was better nourished, with a higher capacity to communicate. Shared narratives were essential to developing and disseminating values, cultures, ideas, stories, and explanations to facilitate cooperation and culture.

From nurseries to campfires, those with a higher capacity to absorb socially accumulated knowledge and who could engage in apprenticeship, teaching, learning, and cooperating had a survival advantage. They could also do something else: play.

Humans could start to tell real and imagined stories for fun around the fire as the sun went down. As linguist Daniel Dor states, "First we invented stories, then they changed us." Increased social engagement, reliance on others, and more time together helped encourage narratives about what was important to our ancestors and who they were.

The use of narratives continues in the modern world, as stories are all around us. Underlying sports, politics, religions, and businesses are stories that unite people around a common purpose, meaning, or identity. Narratives help us make sense of the world and our place in it, creating simplified interpretations and explanations of deeply complex experiences.

The Space Between Stories We Are Told and Those We Create

In the face of instability, we have a drive to make sense of the world. Creating a dance of narratives—stories and explanations—we fill in the blanks for a satisfactory understanding of our experiences as we fumble to answer "Why?" *Why is he doing this? What did they really mean when they said that? Why is this so hard?*

Often, I see the natural longing for human connection manifesting as imagined possibilities—filling in the blanks with stories we eagerly hope to be true. It's common that a highly successful single woman comes into my office with a complex and fantastical story of someone she met and fell in love with after maybe ten minutes. Maybe it was due to a single data point, like being from the same hometown, attending the same university, or having similar struggles in childhood.

Her mind took this data point and created an interwoven web of what their future looked like together: how they'd playfully dance in the kitchen while cleaning up breakfast or how they'd validate each other and both apologize after a conflict. Quickly falling in love with the potential of a person or an idealized image and then crashing into reality a year later causes pain and hurt for all parties involved.

Most people take their past experiences—a first kiss, a graduation ceremony, an embarrassing moment, the first heartbreak or loss—and gradually construct coherent narratives about how they responded, why the situation came to be, and who they are at their core. Over time, this life narrative changes, updates, and autocorrects, layering on a stable sense of identity. In the face of large decisions, we look to our past for inspiration or to remind ourselves about potential dangers to avoid. Stories inform one's sense of self.

We not only fill in the blanks and create stories about how we came to be; we also have ingrained stories that we fall back on during times of instability to explain why something is happening. Some emotionally charged scenes from the past are repeated over and over (that time your mother criticized you publicly or that intense sexual experience with an old fling), and other scenes are left out (the times when your mother doted on you over the holiday or when that same old fling cheated on you). We fill in the blanks of stories to make sense of the world, and we also do it to protect ourselves. Too often, though, the explanations we create aren't what's true but what feels the safest to believe.

The Insecurity Trap

At the age of forty-two, after eight years of blackouts and burned relationships, Chris finally hit rock bottom. At age forty-four, he celebrated twenty-three months of sobriety. Even so, his steadiness felt raw. With an ever-present awareness of the power of one slip to catapult his life back into chaos, he desperately avoided disruption. Although he had always desired a partner, he stayed in his studio apartment, telling himself no one he wanted could ever want someone like *him*. In a desperate act of self-protection, Chris built narrative walls around himself for safety, but those walls also trapped him in isolation and suffering. That is, until he reconnected with a woman during a high-school reunion that his friend dragged him to.

His former high-school girlfriend Elise admired his broody depth, believed in his recovery, and saw potential that he barely recognized in himself. But that's when the script flipped.

The more she encouraged him, the more unworthy he felt. Instead of leaning into her acceptance, he questioned it, testing her and pushing her away. He was obsessed with the belief that one day she'd leave him for someone "on her level," and eventually, she did. Not because he wasn't enough, but because he couldn't believe that he was.

What ended the relationship wasn't only incompatibility—it was the cognitive dissonance between who he was and the story he told himself about who could love him. Trapped in an internalized stereotype, he was certain that he was permanently damaged goods, which brings him into my office.

When I ask why the relationship unraveled, he has a ready explanation: She was manipulative. Controlling. Cold. In his version of the story, he did everything he could—he stayed sober, focused on his work, and read self-help books. But Elise "just never gave me a chance." Chris portrays himself as an underdog hero fighting his own demons while being dragged down by someone who couldn't see his progress.

There is one main problem: Almost none of this narrative is helping him heal. People are bombarded with information in their daily lives, and the most efficient and realistic way to make decisions and protect themselves from harm is to quickly process information and fill in the blanks to create a sense of stability—a sense of knowing. If humans sat and carefully processed all the data thrown at them, our species wouldn't have survived. Instead, we developed an instinctive reflex that rebalances the brain to process information to the best of our ability.

Too often, though, we don't consciously ask ourselves whether our narratives are true. We assume that our first thoughts are accurate. Chris's reflexive explanations are an attempt to protect himself from further pain. Feeling a sense of threat, his nervous system continually pokes him to fight (by telling her how selfish she is) or flight (avoiding her). It's dangerous.

Chris is simmering in a victimhood that patients often have when they enter my clinic. Creating a personal grievance, he needs an underlying threat so his own insecurities make sense and so he can avoid ownership of his own behaviors. The virtuousness of victimhood is appealing and steadies many people slogging through the emotional pits of fragility.

Solidifying his loneliness is a distortion of others' actions, what's termed *externalization of blame*—a defense mechanism in which he pushes uncomfortable truths onto others. He feels in no way responsible for his predicament, externalizing the blame of not finding another romantic partner, sinking into setbacks at work, isolating himself from any social activities—the list of his persuasive reasons as to why he is doomed to depression is endless.

Instead of confronting his flaws, he projects them onto others. While it might protect his ego in the short term, in the long term it erodes self-awareness. Absolving himself of any responsibility for how he's feeling, he holds on to this blame game to solidify his victimhood.

Even when people share genuine compliments or verbalize their love, Chris cannot receive any of it; it's as if he believes he has special powers of knowing the "truth": that he is unlovable. Regardless of how love is given to him, his distortions and insecurity prevent him from receiving any compassion that comes his way.

Whether we are aware of it or not, cognitive-distortion biases such as taking detail out of context, jumping to conclusions, overgeneralization, personalization, all-or-nothing thinking, magnification of the negative and minimization of the positive, and mental filtering abound in us all, shaping the lens through which we view the world and our experiences.

Thinking errors and fear take control, creating instability where there otherwise wouldn't be. Your loyalty to a familiar narrative may keep you from considering a more realistic or nuanced one. The danger isn't in the distortion alone—it's in the repetition. The more often you tell yourself the same story, the more true it feels, whether or not it actually is.

Thankfully, the brain has plasticity, as do our stories and explanations. Rewriting your stories isn't done by erasing the past but by owning your role in it. Accountability begins with curiosity— moving away from *This is what happened to me,* which is where most people land and loiter, to *What have I been telling myself, and why?*

You don't need to be perfect to grow. You just need to question the story that says you do.

Narratives are the playground of psychotherapy. In my sessions with Chris, he uses stories and examples to chase and hide. Over time, I use gentle questioning and curiosity to challenge his thoughts. When feeling down, he jots down his thoughts and sees if they match with a cognitive distortion: *Am I personalizing again? Overgeneralizing?* I help uncover the internal story he uses to define himself. Up until now, that story has been *I've been wronged; I'm always judged; I am a broken human being.*

He starts to shift the narrative to something more empowering: *I'm a failure* becomes *I've made mistakes and am learning. Love is impossible* becomes *I'm learning how to love.* This allows him to practice a powerful approach of decentering—Chris sees his thoughts as just one possible version of reality, not *the* reality.

Cognitive distortions don't disappear by force; they lose their grip through your awareness. The key isn't to suppress distorted thoughts but to interrogate them with curiosity. When you catch yourself thinking, *She doesn't care about me,* pause and ask yourself: *What's the evidence? What else might be true?* This shift from certainty to possibility is called *cognitive reappraisal*—interpreting a thought or event in a more balanced way.

Over time, the brain starts to recognize these distortions as familiar old scripts, not immutable truths. The shift isn't about thinking positively but about thinking more accurately. Challenging cognitive distortions helps you rethink the stories you tell yourself. But sometimes, the real distortion isn't in what you're thinking—it's in what you're not feeling.

How Are You Feeling?

Affect theorist Silvan Tomkins points out that there are three main forces responsible for motivating change: biological drives (such as thirst, hunger, and sex), physical pain, and affect (the raw, unconscious reaction that happens before you even label what you're experiencing). Of these, affects, which are closely related to emotions and feelings, are the most influential in changing behavior, as they modulate our experiences. Excitement energizes an experience, while shame stifles it. We can't change basic drives of thirst and hunger, but we can reshape what we've been taught to fear or feel ashamed of.

Our emotions are a critical leverage point in our lives, as they are a fundamental force in motivating our narratives. Most emotions connected to experiences have been learned, which is good news, as it means they can also be changed. Instead of being anxiety-ridden in an intimate relationship, you can learn to be joyful. It's possible to become less afraid or ashamed in your anger or sadness.

The challenge is, most people don't know what they're feeling at any given time. If they do notice an internal cue, they don't have the language to know what they're feeling beyond *good, fine,* or *bad.* If you aren't aware of your increasing anger, sadness, or tenderness, then you'll continue to develop stories and explanations that may not be aligned with reality or your best interest, ultimately creating more suffering and instability.

I often have people come to me stating they have a conflict between "head and heart." "My head is telling me she's perfect, but my heart is telling me she's not the one for me" or "My heart is telling me to pursue this passion, but my head is telling me that's ridiculous." Or they agonize because of the perception that others have undervalued or disrespected them. They try to square the circle by developing mantras or lists of affirmations to help bridge the gap: *My body is strong and beautiful! I believe in myself! I deserve happiness!*

While I love seeing affirmations posted on people's bathroom mirrors and refrigerators and delivered on daily apps, I don't typically prescribe them. Day to day, they aren't harmful, and if they work for you, by all means, partake. While affirmations can offer a moment of comfort or motivation, I haven't seen them, on their own, lead to deep or lasting change in those that walk through my office door. I find them to be aspirational—they tell us how we want to feel.

That's because positive self-statements can be a form of gaslighting. Let's say you're struggling with feeling disrespected and demeaned. You want to believe that you are valuable and unique, so you tell yourself *I am worthy* every morning. You may find hope and even hold your belief for thirty seconds. But most likely, after those precious seconds pass, you can easily conjure up a longer list of reasons why you are *not* worthy than why you *are*.

Instead of telling yourself you're worthy, think of a specific time when you felt valued and allow yourself the space to *feel* the emotion. You're much more likely to internalize and integrate the sense of being valued if you tie it to an experience and feeling of being valued. Unless you link the statement with authentic emotion and actions, the words won't stick.

Affect Phobia

From the time she was in kindergarten, Hannah knew she was going to be outstanding when she grew up. She was told as much. Becoming a prominent lawyer or CEO of a company wasn't out of her reach—both her parents were Ivy League–educated and nationally recognized. But that didn't protect them from upheaval.

Her father, a graduate of one of the top business schools in the United States, was a real estate tycoon, but he made some poor investment choices and lost millions within a year. Panic, blame, and wounds to the ego now filled every corner of Hannah's home. With only one sibling, a brother who was constantly reprimanded at school, Hannah was the golden child; she would be the one to restore the family's reputation and prestige.

Hannah rose to the challenge—she had no other choice. Realizing that predicting and meeting others' needs made her feel important, after school, Hannah helped tutor her classmates. Dirty clothes were never an issue for her family members—Hannah was always on top of the laundry. She pursued fencing, a strategic sport that required her to identify how others thought in order to outmaneuver them.

Mature for her age, Hannah wore her responsibility with pride, but with the pressure of earning straight As, running for student-body president, and becoming editor of the school newspaper, Hannah reached a breaking point. The pride and fun that she once felt in her activities were overshadowed by the need to achieve, and yet she couldn't allow herself to stop.

Today Hannah is the president of a multibillion-dollar marketing and communication business. Now in her mid-forties, she drags herself into my office, struggling with a constant sense of personal and professional instability. She is set on being promoted to chief executive officer—she wants it all. In Hannah's short four months at the company, multiple executives have told her how impressed and happy they are with her work.

Despite this, Hannah feels like a failure. Even when she receives praise, she is able to absorb it only temporarily, the next day grabbing new projects in an anxious frenzy to prove her worth. When she sees her former teammates working on successful projects, she wants not only to be part of that success but to take ownership of it.

Instead of transitioning fully into her new role, Hannah co-opts her colleagues' projects, then becomes overwhelmed and resentful that people are not giving her as much recognition as she needs. She becomes demanding, harsh, and condescending to those around her.

"I know what I'm doing, but I can't let go. I've got this narrative in my head that I'm not good enough—that people are going to see the real me and learn I'm not actually that smart. I think the praise is just because they are trying to be nice. They don't actually think I'm capable of doing the job," she concludes.

Power of the Missing

Hannah is aware of her social narratives and cognitive distortions and tries to change her perspective and her unhelpful ways of thinking. Yet she struggles with feeling any meaningful internal change. Anxiety, shame, and fear inflame her nervous system on a daily basis. Like a trick birthday candle, flames momentarily wane but then quickly reappear.

While I listen for potential hidden narratives, I also search for missing emotions. Specifically, emotions that she might be terrified of experiencing. This is what Harvard psychologist Leigh McCullough calls *affect phobia*—a maladaptive fear of certain feelings.

There are some people who relate past difficulties in their lives in stories stripped of feeling. They unemotionally tell stories about the loss of a loved one, living in unsafe conditions, or violations, and by playing this recording over and over, they believe they have "dealt with" the past. Yet if you don't see the feelings associated with an event, you don't see a part of yourself. You can't fully bear witness to an event without bearing witness to the associated pain and suffering.

While Hannah doesn't allow herself to acknowledge the deep pain of being emotionally abandoned by her parents, she does allow herself to feel—and intensely! Anxiety and anger abound throughout her personal and professional relationships. "I know I'm super-anxious about doing a good job—my review was positive, but I can't feel it. At some point, I know they're going to find out I'm a fraud. I'm not as good as they think I am." Anxiety is Hannah's path of least resistance, the most familiar emotion she allows herself to sink into.

When I look for missing emotions in her narrative, I'm not hunting for a general lack of feeling. I'm searching for the specific feelings that are being protected—feelings that she might not even be aware of.

Tending to the Porcupine

I introduce Hannah to her porcupine. Generally affectionate and intelligent animals, porcupines love to snuggle and rub their noses on you. When threatened, the porcupine raises its thirty thousand sharp quills to protect its soft underbelly, bare face, and legs. Like porcupines, humans use our defensive behaviors like quills to protect ourselves from emotions we don't want to experience. Reflexively engaging in defensive thoughts, behaviors, or emotions such as anxiety, guilt, shame, or pain protects us from touching upon something terrifying.

You can become trapped by your own emotions when you ignore or suppress feelings to avoid pain, discomfort, or vulnerability. This avoidance of emotions can stem from a deep-seated belief that emotions are inherently dangerous or overwhelming.

But here's the kicker: While avoidance can provide you with temporary relief, it ultimately keeps you stuck, because the very emotions you're trying to avoid end up controlling you from behind the scenes. Other phobias are treated with exposure therapy, and my approach to this one is gradual emotional exposure. My aim is to help Hannah experience emotions in a mindful way so she can see them not as threats but as normal and manageable aspects of being human.

I ask Hannah to describe a specific recent example of a time when she felt out of control. "I was invited to speak at a large industry conference. They introduced me with a glowing bio that made it sound like I had transformed the organization." Pride tiptoes into her eyes but stands back, hesitant. "The team was really happy about this and made a big deal of it at our executive meeting, but I secretly felt like a fraud. I couldn't enjoy it because I was so scared of being found out."

Hannah uses shame defensively—it is her reflexive quill that flares outward, though it hurts her the most. The question then becomes: What's the role of her shame? What are her quills protecting her from? In that soft underbelly, she holds positive feelings toward herself—self-confidence, pride, esteem, self-compassion. Why is she so phobic about feeling positively toward herself?

Growing up, Hannah learned that she would not be loved if she had certain emotions and responses. Her high-achieving parents played Whac-A-Mole with her emotions, squashing those that they weren't comfortable with, like anger, sorrow, and excitement, and shaming her for asserting her desires and needs. She learned that feeling proud of herself came at a cost—it meant she was being arrogant, entitled, and conceited.

Feeling proud of herself meant losing the love of her parents, so shame became a clear way to block that conflict. Shame told her she was unworthy of praise so she didn't have to contend with the pain of losing her parents' love if she showed high self-regard. She has created a well-trodden path to shame that she races down in response to any positive feelings about herself.

Exposing the Underbelly

Since many emotional responses operate outside of conscious awareness, we can first examine the behaviors that might be causing disruption in our lives. Typically, defensive behaviors are those that drive others away or shut you down: passivity and withdrawal, silencing, acting out, rushing through conversations, smiling when discussing something painful, forgetting appointments, being overly sarcastic or passive-aggressive, quickly changing the subject, or overintellectualizing and rationalizing.

These behaviors can create more havoc than we realize, but they are serving a purpose: to protect. Defining what your porcupine quills are allows you to ask what they are protecting—what's in the underbelly?

Once you clarify what emotions you are terrified to engage in, you can gradually allow exposure. Just like any other phobia, such as a fear of flying or riding elevators, an exposure approach treats the fear of a specific feeling. When you give a sweet smile or act politely toward someone who has demeaned or offended you, you might understand your quills to be placating and fawning to protect from your rage and anger toward that person.

People are often surprised by the most common feelings hidden in our underbellies. Emotions are often labeled good or bad, positive or negative. Many are raised to believe that anger and fear are bad; joy and tenderness are good. Yet emotions exist on a spectrum with many dimensions. Fear can lead to the downfall of a promising relationship, or it can shield you from a potentially harmful partner. As Leigh McCullough points out, rather than categorizing emotions as good or bad, we can view them as helpful (encouraging healthy behaviors) or maladaptive (hindering personal growth).

In essence, ask yourself: Does fear guide you to engage in constructive ways with yourself and others, or does it become destructive, worsening your feelings about yourself and those around you?

Yes, Hannah feels anxiety when she's praised, but that anxiety dances with shame that she's unworthy of praise, protecting her from any positive feelings about herself. Her shame is inhibiting and maladaptive—it serves to make her shut down and withdraw. She's terrified of truly experiencing positive regard for herself, a helpful feeling that could activate her to engage with herself and others in a healthier manner.

Desperate longing for daily recognition and affirmation from her boss is due to a lack of pride, self-confidence, and self-esteem. Hannah's need for validation from others becomes exaggerated. And she's not alone. Many people do this in romantic relationships— crave another person as a way to validate that one is indeed lovable.

Understanding Hannah's porcupine self allows her to engage in a gradual exposure to that which she's scared of: positive self-regard. She learned that being confident and proud of herself was arrogant and foolish. Scared of her own entitlement to individual needs and wants, she has made shame her default zone. Historically, this has come at a high cost: isolation, perpetual dissatisfaction, and inner turmoil.

Over our sessions, Hannah opens up to the missing emotion that remained tucked away in the corner. Slowly but surely, she allows herself to feel pride, decoupling it from shame. The most important driver to her success is a shift in perspective: Emotions aren't the enemy—they're the messengers. What we call affect phobia isn't a flaw; it's simply something we learned to do to protect ourselves. The good news? It can be unlearned. When you turn toward your feelings instead of away from them, you give yourself the chance for more freedom and richer connection with others. The goal isn't to let emotions take over your life but to befriend them and let them guide you. Emotional avoidance might a habit, but emotional courage can be too.

Action Tools for Story of Stories

A. Break Free from Cultural-Identity Traps

1. Name the script you've inherited. We often talk about beliefs as if they're choices, but many of them are inherited scripts. Until we examine the script, we can't choose a different role. Cultural norms often run in stealth mode. Pause and ask yourself: *What roles have I been expected to play, and who wrote that script?*

2. Differentiate internal values from external expectations. Challenge the false link between identity and worth. You aren't more valuable because you self-sacrifice or less valuable because you ask for help. Worth isn't earned by suffering. What do *you* believe makes a good parent, leader, or partner? Clarity about your own values is the first step to rewriting the role.

3. Practice identity experimentation. Transformation begins by trying on new behaviors *before* you fully believe you can own them. Redefine strength as flexibility, not endurance. Strength isn't sticking to one role no matter the cost. It's having the agility to evolve as your life changes.

4. Rewrite your role. Identify your inherited narrative, and instead of repeating it, replace it with a new one. For example, forgo the inherited narrative "A good mother puts herself last" in favor of a new one: "A sustainable mother includes herself in the equation."

B. Rewrite Your Inner Narrative

5. Spot your go-to distortions. Over time, repeated thought patterns become invisible rules for how to interpret reality. Cognitive distortions aren't a sign of weakness; they're mental shortcuts you've outgrown. Start a daily practice of catching and naming your top patterns, like all-or-nothing thinking, mind-reading, catastrophizing, and emotional reasoning.

6. Decenter your thoughts. Thoughts aren't truths; they're drafts. Just because a thought arrives in your mind doesn't mean it de-

serves airtime. The most confident minds are the ones willing to revise their first assumptions. When a distressing thought pops up, write it down and list two to three alternate interpretations. Treat your thoughts like hypotheses, not conclusions.

7. Shift from blame to responsibility. Blame feels good in the moment but robs you of growth. While it keeps the story simple, it also keeps you powerless. Responsibility doesn't mean you caused the problem. It means you're claiming your role in solving it. Replace *Who caused this?* with *What's my role in this?* or *What part of this can I do differently next time?*

8. Separate emotional volume from emotional truth. Emotions often pose as facts, but they aren't the final word. They are signals, not verdicts. We assume if we feel something strongly, it must be true, but just because it's intense doesn't mean it's accurate. When gripped with emotion, ask yourself: *What is this feeling trying to protect me from?* Then look for one piece of evidence that challenges the story your emotion is telling.

9. Replace certainty with curiosity. Certainty keeps us comfortable; curiosity keeps us growing. The best minds don't cling to being right but stay open to being surprised. Updating your narratives integrates your past with a commitment to your future. Ask yourself: *What's one part of my story that needs a rewrite?*

C. Tend to Your Porcupine

10. Name the emotion to tame it. You can't manage what you don't recognize, and emotions lose their grip when we name them. Instead of letting vague discomfort cloud your thinking, pause and ask yourself: *What exactly am I feeling now?* Labeling an emotion, like *anxious, hurt,* or *excited,* helps engage the rational brain and lowers emotional overwhelm.

11. Spot the avoidance patterns. Emotional avoidance is invisible until you look for it. Most people don't even realize they're avoiding. Do you make jokes when the conversation gets serious? Shut down when you're hurt? Intellectualize when you're uncomfortable? These are subtle defenses. Track when you're shifting away due to emotional discomfort—that's the entry point to change.

12. Challenge the internal rules. We are taught early on to fear or suppress certain emotions that are "bad." But emotional rules like *Anger is dangerous* and *Vulnerability is weakness* are often outdated survival strategies. Ask yourself: *Is this belief helping me or holding me back?* Start by replacing inherited beliefs with healthier ones. For example, *It's okay to feel angry without losing control.*

13. Replace defenses with emotional expression. Defenses keep us safe as well as stuck. When you catch yourself deflecting, whether through sarcasm, silence, or perfection, try swapping in honest emotional language. Take small emotional risks. You overcome affect phobia as you would any phobia—with exposure therapy. Gradually face the emotions you fear in safe doses. For example, if expressing anger scares you, start by saying, "I'm frustrated," instead of pretending that everything is fine.

2

Memories

As an adult, I carry my father's death like an empty purse. I try to pack it with photos and stories, but they aren't my own. So I'm left with the fragile memories of a teenager, stripped of the possibility of seeing my father through adult eyes. Overexposed photos capture how I perceived him at the time: annoying, distant, and kind. Adding texture to his personality is hard, as there aren't new experiences to fine-tune my understanding of him.

I remember snapshot images of my father after his assault: Recounting his kidnapping attack to a friend as I sat outside his hospital room. Covering bruises and stab wounds that tattooed his torso. Shaving his head over a pink vomit bin, him sighing with relief from the itching. Him flinching in compassionate annoyance when I filled his plastic hospital pitcher with ice but tripped and dumped it all over him in his bed.

Wanting something to remember him by, I placed a mini–tape recorder by the side of his bed, hoping he would be inspired to leave pearls of wisdom. Breaths quickly replaced dwindling words, as he had to struggle to breathe, let alone speak. These are the only memories I have within reach because he passed away after a few weeks in hospice care.

I knew the events of that time, but I didn't know the story. Wanting to better understand the circumstances around my father's death,

I searched for clues or details that could give me a better sense of what happened during the assault. A clip in the local newspaper reported that the judge overseeing the trial of the men accused of assaulting my father said, "Even if he recovers from the injury, he will never recover from that episode." But he didn't recover—or did he?

When I did a deeper dive into the basic facts of my father's death, including the exact dates of all the events—the assault in February 1993, the hospitalization and his death in March 1994, I learned that my memory of him never returning home after the assault and staying in hospice for six weeks until his death was incorrect.

What I have recently learned is that while the details of the assault and kidnapping were correct, he was the victim of an *attempted* murder, not an actual one. The trauma of his assault and kidnapping and the ambiguity of whether he would live froze my memory for a year.

After the assault, he was released from the shock trauma unit and discharged home, where he lived for a year. He was then diagnosed with metastatic cancer, admitted to the hospital, and quickly transferred to hospice, where he died after three weeks.

I clearly remember the bookends of this period—the assault and his stay in hospice—but the time in between went missing. *Did I eat dinner with him every night? Did I still play piano for him? Maybe we laughed about his dad jokes, and perhaps I rolled my eyes when he commented on how tight my top was.* If someone told me that these things happened, I could incorporate them into my suggestible narrative. But I'm not sure. All these details were blocked from my psyche.

During my high-school and even college years, I can't say that I believed he'd died from the assault. There simply was no narrative, no discussions within my family or with others. I glided on the surface.

Your subconscious creatively works to order experiences into a resonant structure so they'll fit your worldview. I fell into this trap. A desperation for stability and a sense of knowing paired with the neurobiological effects of trauma to create a simplified narrative that gave me a clean explanation for his death.

Over time, the psychological trauma on my memory shaped a narrative of his gruesome death by murder. True to the cultural shifts toward sound bites and the natural instinct to simplify explanations, I concluded, and believed, my dad had been murdered.

Memories Are for Meaning

We are taught that our brains are like video cameras, capturing literal, objective facts about our experiences. *They are just wrong—they aren't remembering it correctly!* Relationships are pummeled with hurts and grievances due to differences in how each person remembers what happened.

Children are taught in schools to memorize facts, from the names of the presidents to math theories to the history of the escalation of wars. Being able to memorize fixed information is seen as a sign of intelligence. As you move through the world, this framework underlies your perceptions: Your memories are recorded facts that are etched into your brain. If you want to know what really happened, you just need to access the right mental video.

Yet we all have limited versions of the world. We think we see everything in its entirety, but the truth is, we're just darting our eyes around and filling in the rest of the story or explanation with memories. Memories are integrated into stories when we tell people about the first time a baby laughed and a funny incident at the last family gathering. We need memories to function in the world; they help us develop our narratives to understand the past, inform the present, and predict the future.

Some of these memories are pushed so far out of your consciousness that you no longer have awareness of them. Perhaps you've forgotten about times long ago when you were bullied by peers or neglected by family, or maybe you have a general sense of your parents' love being conditional on your good behavior but you can't remember specific details.

Memories are a powerful force in developing narratives. Your perceptions of what you believe you have been are the basis of your identity and tell you who you are. Over the past two decades, social science research has found evidence that the way people tell their own narratives has implications for their mental health and well-being.

I remember speaking with a former child soldier who told me, "I never killed anyone innocent, just people who deserved it." His language around the memories of his time with the rebel group was used to maintain self-esteem and avoid guilt, shaping who he believed himself to be. We tell stories not because we need to remember but because we need to remember something that fits.

We use our memories to explain the past, clarify the present, and get a fuzzy glimpse into the future. They define us and shape our identities and ways of perceiving the world. Your mind is like a detective—you have one clue and you have to use your best guesses and past experiences to fill in the gaps and make a narrative of what happened. Shaping how you behave, memories influence your responses to cues in your environment, and affect how you recover from adversity.

Memories are so powerful that even a certain smell can evoke a sense of vulnerability, chaos, violation, and insecurity or nostalgia, peace, comfort, and love. How you remember is a critical aspect of how you author your narratives. Your moods shape how you remember past experiences. Your identity directs your attention to what you should remember. And your self-interest steers your interpretation of what happened and how you responded.

Since memories are so foundational to one's sense of self, they're worth attending to. Rarely do people question whether their memories are accurate. The default is to believe they are factual, complete, and robust. But how can you be sure that your memories are telling you the truth, and what do you do when you can't remember?

Fragments of Memory

One morning in his room, a young man stared at the Bible sitting next to his bed. Saturated with frustration, he massaged his head and paced his cell. José was sixteen years old, and this was his third immigration custody placement in four months. Without the care of an adult figure, he was one of the 76,000 unaccompanied children who traveled across the southern US border searching for a safe haven in 2019.

Holding the Bible to his chest, he willed himself to remember his mother. After all, she was the one who'd given it to him. It was one of the few mementos he had of her—she had passed away four years ago from cancer. Born and raised in Honduras, José lived with his father and sisters after his mother died. While he remembered moments of childhood—playing tag, learning how to build homes with his father, and riding his bike around town—the rest of his childhood was relatively blank.

After José's mother died, his father turned to drinking and drugs, forcing José to drop out of school and work in construction to support the family. Two years earlier, during a drunken argument, his father had kicked him out of the house, and José found himself on the streets with nowhere to sleep. Within a week, he was lured by a former neighbor, then threatened, drugged, and trafficked for sexual exploitation with little access to food or water until the police rescued him during an undercover sting operation three months later.

In the hallway after the raid, officers tried to get the basics—his name, if anyone was still inside, how many men there were. One impatient officer leaned in, voice tight. "Give us something. What happened in there?" José stared, unable to answer. Wanting to help, he muttered, "They drank Imperial beer—from the bottles, with caps." When pressed, he gave his best guess of where he had been and what had happened, information that was later found to be incorrect.

Child protection authorities coordinated with a local nongovernmental organization to bring him to a shelter, but when word reached him that men from the neighborhood were asking about him, fear outweighed safety. José, alone and carrying the burden of a weight larger than his life, turned away from the shelter in self-reproach. Drinking out of bathroom sinks and eating from trash cans and mango trees, José traveled by foot and bus to the United States.

Now he sits across a table from me in juvenile detention as I conduct a psychological evaluation for his asylum claim. His lawyer pulls me aside. "Find out why he didn't just stay in safety when he could have. Why didn't he stay at the shelter? Why didn't he cooperate with the local police and give them the information they were asking for?" Unfortunately, José is equally confused by his behavior and is upset with himself for not being able to explain his actions.

I've worked with many survivors across the spectrum of despair over the years, and I've become more and more humble to neurobiology. Plenty of people, including those in law enforcement, social services, and health services, assume that memory is merely a matter of replaying the past, that survivors can remember everything accurately.

Yet the truth is, our memories are far less accurate than we believe. The brain is not like a container that holds data. If you were to zoom in on your brain while you're forming a memory, you'd see fireworks—a burst of electrical activity lighting up a network of neurons. That's how memories begin—as connections, not containers.

When you form a memory, your brain isn't storing a snapshot; it's playing a tennis match. At the neural level, memory begins when neurons (your brain's messengers) start hitting the ball back and forth across the synapse, the tiny gap between them. These tennis balls are chemical messengers (neurotransmitters) that keep the game going. Tennis partners improve their rhythm and precision with practice, and neurons operate the same way—the more often they communicate, the stronger and faster the connection becomes. This process turns a casual game into a high-speed match, and it's one of the brain's core methods for encoding lasting memories.

But memories aren't confined to a single court. They're built across networks of brain regions, each area handling a different part of the experience: sights, sounds, emotions, and context. As the memory gets practiced and refined, the players—the neurons—need less guidance, a process termed *consolidation*.

Here's the fascinating twist: Every time you remember something, it's not an instant replay of the exact event. The brain opens up the memory, subtly adjusts it based on new conditions, such as mood, context, and knowledge, and reconsolidates the updated version. In other words, your tennis game is shaped by practice, influenced by others, and always evolving to help you navigate what's next.

If you were asked what happened on your last vacation, you probably wouldn't offer a chronological report of the events. Most likely, you would respond with "It was so beautiful!" or "It was so refreshing, I want to go back next year." That summary is based on how your cortex integrated data points and developed a coherent story—it evaluated the overall impression and organized a narrative into episodic memory, the memory formed through experience.

If you don't have an engaged prefrontal cortex, you're left with fragments of data that may or may not appear connected, and the story of your vacation will confuse both yourself and your listener.

Thankfully, not all information gets encoded into memory—that would be inefficient and cumbersome. What is encoded is a function of what you pay attention to. Whether you're reading the words on this page, having a conversation, or learning how to play the piano, your prefrontal cortex helps you decide what to focus on.

How We Forget

Your limbic system, the innermost part of your brain, serves as the emotional seat of the brain and pairs with the prefrontal cortex to create a coherent narrative. When you're scared, surprised, disgusted, or intrigued, neuromodulators—chemicals such as dopamine, noradrenaline, cortisol, and serotonin—are released, and they affect what you pay attention to and the connections between your neurons. When a large furry animal is coming toward you, you want to quickly assess what it is, based on your memory of what a bear looks like and what a dog looks like.

When a person is in a high-arousal state (such as the life-threatening situations that José experienced), the amygdala of the limbic system fires and takes priority. When you're faced with highly stressful or life-threatening conditions, it's hard to consider anything other than where your attention is focused—on survival.

José's neurobiology did what it was supposed to—it activated his survival mechanism. When the fear circuitry is activated, the rational prefrontal cortex is muted, and any information that's relevant to survival is encoded as central information. For José, details about a beer bottle were more important than details about his abductors, because the bottle could be used as a weapon and therefore was threatening to his life.

When people are in high-stress conditions, contextual information, like the layout of a room or the sequence of certain events, becomes peripheral and is poorly encoded—it's not essential to survival. This isn't a conscious choice but a normal process that the brain undergoes during extremely stressful situations.

Police officers, soldiers, and people who have been attacked or feared for their lives likely all had similar experiences. And after the fear settles down, the hippocampus goes into overdrive, remembering in exquisite detail what happened right before and right after the trauma, though the memories are likely fragmented and incomplete.

Why is this important to understand? Because neurobiology suggests that many common responses to difficult situations are involuntary and due to fear and trauma, not deliberate deception. José's questionable actions created doubt in the interrogator's mind but also in his own. He began to internalize anger and shame that he didn't fight back, try to escape, or pay attention to important details. *How can I not remember?* he thinks. *I don't even know who I am anymore. I can't even explain a story about my life.*

José has been chastising himself hourly for not being able to create a coherent narrative because of his lack of clear memory about the past. Parts of his brain shut down in order for him to survive and manage. *Dissociative amnesia* is the clinical term for this phenomenon. His memory loss was a natural survival skill, a defense mechanism against psychological harm. But it has left him confused, uncertain, and untrusting of himself.

If José cannot offer any clear memories, his asylum application is at risk. The burden of proof of persecution for an asylum seeker is the same whether the person is a child or an adult. But developmentally, children struggle to categorize their experiences into legally useful narratives. It's hard for children to coherently state linear and reflective narratives showing that their experiences were traumatic and deserving of attention.

Instead of focusing on the exact memory, I help José understand his own neurobiology and explain that his reactions were a completely normal response, that his brain was doing what it had to do to keep him alive. In the context of something so overwhelming and hard to make sense of, everyone is hardwired to forget or misremember.

When I work with him, I help him manage his response when he remembers the inhumane parts of his past. I'm not helping him unlearn a response. I'm helping him learn how to suppress the association with fear. The hippocampus (memory center), amygdala (fear center), and prefrontal cortex (thinking center) are all working together to say, *You're okay right now, in this office, in this context.*

When something triggers him, though—a memory evoked by an external stimulus, like smelling the familiar scent of his abuser or seeing a man wearing a shirt similar to his abuser's—his brain chemistry changes. Neurotransmitters are released to activate a particular mental context or state of mind that opens the windows to past memories.

This lapse of memory during traumatic events isn't unusual; it's a normal response of the brain. But it's not just traumatic events that cause memory lapses. We are all subject to the machinations of memory. We don't need to experience life-threatening events to have moments of forgetfulness; it's happened to all of us: *Where did I put the keys? What time is my appointment?* When we think about memory issues, we often think about how we forget. It's easy to focus on incomplete memories due to missing facts of the past. Equally influential, though, is how we remember.

Memory as a Process of Reconstruction

Imagine you're rewatching a movie you haven't seen in years. You remember the plot, the big twist, maybe even something the main character wore. But halfway through, something odd happens: You're sure a scene is missing. Wasn't there a part where the detective breaks down crying? You remember it so clearly, but it's not there. You didn't forget something. You invented something.

Psychologist Daniel Schacter has a list of what he calls the "sins of memory," and this is one of them: suggestibility. You aren't gullible or weak-minded; your brain is an efficient storyteller and doesn't like blank spaces. When memory falters, the brain fills in the blanks, not randomly but by using context, expectation, and your prior knowledge of the world. Your brain isn't trying to deceive you; it's just trying to make sense of the past.

One of Schacter's most elegant demonstrations of this involved the Deese-Roediger-McDermott (DRM) task, a deceptively simple memory test. Participants were given a list of related words, such as *bed, rest, tired, dream, night, snooze,* then asked to recall as many as they could. The researchers found that most participants confidently remembered hearing the word *sleep,* even though it was not on the list.

Why? Their brains inferred the missing link. *Sleep* fit the theme so well that the mind treated it as fact. This wasn't about being inattentive; it was about the brain finding coherence, even if it meant bending the truth.

The gaps in your memory are filled in with assumptions, stories, and, sometimes, borrowed fragments from TV shows, conversations, or things that happened to someone else entirely. Nobel Prize winner Daniel Kahneman calls this the "remembering self" —it's the narrative-builder part of the mind that cares more about the story making sense than about getting every detail right. So the next time you're arguing with your friend about that vacation and whether she *did* walk on the beach with you, remember, your brain isn't lying. It's storytelling on your behalf.

We all distort memories in this way, even when we're trying to be honest. This process of remembering may say more about who someone wants to be than about what actually happened. Memory distortions often appear deceitful, but I have come to respect the depth of desire they hide. As Emily Dickinson wrote, "The Brain—is wider than the Sky." Reconstructing memories is an expansive process.

Collective Memories: Public Versus Private

Alex drove down the winding road to the town where he'd grown up and felt his body tense before he even reached the familar streets. Instead of pulling into the parking lot for his high school reunion he went to a nearby diner, where two classmates were waiting. At twenty-four years old, Alex had a toddler, a full-time job, and a box of yearbook photos he didn't remember posing for. His adolescence was a blur. "It's like I've read about my teenage years instead of lived it," he said.

Over coffee, his friends brought up events he had no memory of. "Do you remember the night of senior prom, when you disappeared for hours?" one asked. Alex didn't. He looked at them, confused. The other added gently, "You always seemed distracted or checked out back then. We worried about you."

Alex sat in silence. The gap between their memories and his own was destabilizing—what do you do when someone else remembers your life better than you do?

As he walked through the familiar halls of the school, all he felt was emptiness. *What happened within these walls? How did it affect me?* He knew that his best friend had died in a sudden car accident but couldn't remember specifics. The days and months afterward were a haze. He remembered snippets: silence at the lunch table, teachers lowering their voices, but the rest was blurred.

What brings him to my office isn't just confusion—it's the fear hidden in the question: *What really happened to me?*

With his friend no longer alive to help piece things together,

Alex tried to reconstruct his teenage years through the fragments that others carried. Wandering through each hallway, he searched for any images, clues, smells, or trinkets that could spark his memory of what happened. Without those memories, he felt incomplete.

Neuroscientists have long known that trauma can interfere with memory formation, especially when it happens early in life. The brain's job in moments of fear isn't to record but to protect.

And yet, memory is a social act. For Alex, talking with his friends didn't just add information—it created context. Psychologist William Hirst calls this "collaborative remembering," a process in which people reconstruct the past together.

Alex filled in the gaps of his high school years by creating memories that made sense of what was missing. His memories didn't return in high-definition, but the emotional truth of his adolescence—the fear, tension, and silence—began to feel more real. What we remember is partly based on the thing we're remembering, but it's also shaped by what we're familiar with, who we are sharing with, and what images we see.

The truth is, memory is a mosaic made from moments and meanings, shaped by what we lived and by how others witnessed us living it. And, like any mosaic, its form changes depending on who's helping lay the tiles.

All of this means we should be deliberate about whom we engage with, aware of how questioning and discussion could lead to steering a loved one down a certain path. Past images can take on new significance in the context of current events. Memories about a situation can even change based on the representations and images of the situation. The same person can be portrayed as an honorable soldier or a passive participant in a meaningless conflict, depending on public sentiment. Memorials, commemorative holidays, and the media all influence how, when, and what one remembers. In other words, memory is both deeply personal and unavoidably social.

So how do you protect yourself from the constant reshaping and influencing of others on your memories? Alex already took the first step. One of the best ways to combat distorted memories is to be aware of their fragility. Open-ended questions and balanced discussions with people you trust can also help prevent memory distortions.

Alex and I discuss the influence of others in strengthening, distorting, and even overwriting individual memories, and we shift the goal from uncovering memories to validating his current emotional experience. Alex is aware that he must choose his co-rememberers wisely, leaning on those who can offer clarity instead of conclusions.

Since Alex will never know the specific details of what happened long ago, I help him shift away from pressuring himself to recover clear memories and toward allowing himself permission not to know.

In a form of radical acceptance, Alex begins to embrace the idea that not all gaps in his memory need to be filled, that the absence of memory doesn't equate to a missing truth. He begins to focus on understanding who he is now and how his present self has been shaped by his past, whether remembered or not.

Regardless of the details, Alex is clear that what lingers is not a memory but a feeling: a heaviness in his chest, a fog in his mind, and a weariness that settles in whenever he thinks back to those years. Anchoring his healing in what he *does* know—the emotional truth of his loss—can be more liberating than trying to reconstruct every missing moment. Letting go of the need to force a definitive narrative has allowed him to move toward acceptance and self-compassion; he is no longer bound by the need for a perfect narrative of his life.

There are times, though, when the issue isn't forgetting—it's not being able to forget. For those who have experienced major dangers or ruptures to the sense of self, it may be hard to forget certain experiences despite their best efforts. There might be times when they want to talk about what happened to them but they are blocked from publicly discussing it, as doing so might cause discomfort to others. Memory, then, becomes a form of resistance and repair.

Memory: Resistance and Repair

Gabriela, affectionately called "Gabs" by friends, surprised those around her when she chose to attend a small liberal arts college across the country. With a passion for creative writing, she dreamed of becoming a novelist. But as the daughter of teachers who had worked multiple jobs to afford her education, she understood how fortunate she was to be there and wanted to make the most of it. Gabriela was aware that college would challenge her academically and socially. What she wasn't aware of was how unsafe it could become.

One afternoon, Gabriela was working on a group project. When the meeting ended, everyone left except one senior who lingered around, joking about her writing before suddenly closing the distance between them. When she froze and tried to leave, he blocked the door. The assault happened quickly, without witnesses, in a quiet study room where her cries went unheard.

Nearly one in four college women reports experiencing sexual assault before graduation, and many more never tell anyone, silenced by fear, disbelief, or shame. Though campuses have expanded their Title IX offices (the federally mandated programs that handle sexual misconduct cases) and consent education, the culture often remains one where reputation eclipses accountability. Such was the case for Gabriela.

After the assault, she went to the bathroom and scrubbed her skin raw. She didn't consider calling campus security, nor did she know what would happen if she did. She avoided the library where she might see him, dropped her favorite class, and drifted through days in a fog. Weeks later, encouraged by another student who had endured a similar assault, Gabriela filed a formal complaint.

Under university policy, her complaint triggered an investigation with interviews, document reviews, and a hearing panel. The process dragged on for months. She was asked to recount the assault repeatedly. He was a varsity athlete and president of a student organization, well known on campus, and continued attending classes and team events as though nothing had happened. In the end, the panel ruled there was insufficient evidence to determine a violation— there were no witnesses or physical proof—he had good character references, and she had little proof. The panel noted that his behavior seemed "out of character" and closed the case.

In the face of this helplessness, Gabriela tried her best to ignore the initial violation as well as the ongoing institutional abandonment. She tried to push aside memories of what happened when the rightful anger coursing through her body became trapped with seemingly nowhere to go.

Gabriela learned that several others had reported him privately but had been discouraged from filing formal complaints. Together, they began collecting stories and circulated an anonymous online list naming alleged assailants who still moved freely on campus. The list spread quickly, sparking outrage and uncomfortable conversations about safety and power.

The administration was thrust into a dilemma, caught between protecting students and preserving the college's image. Their public statement praised the courage of survivors but avoided acknowledging how procedures built for neutrality can still favor those with power. Despite exhaustion and grief, Gabriela refused to disappear. What began as one night of devastation turned into a campus reckoning that revealed not just individual harm but the quiet failures of an institution built to protect its own.

Gabriela was able to make her memories public but was met with injustice. Others aren't able to. The memories are too painful to relay to others, including themselves. These hidden transcripts of memory carry both horror and loss, some of which people allow themselves to see and others that stay dormant. Many people turn away from the past in order to survive in the present. They don't want to think about or put words to what happened.

Most people I know who have suffered from injustice, violation, or abuses try to hide their hurtful experiences. As they fall more and more into isolation, shame quickly follows. Without anywhere useful to go, anger becomes directed inward into self-loathing and the belief that one is a burden on others. Despite survivors' conscious attempts not to remember, memories find insidious ways to communicate what's happened.

Ruminations, nightmares, bad dreams, a sense of being on edge or jittery, tense muscles, and difficulty focusing are all ways in which painful memories are embodied. The clinical term *post-traumatic stress disorder* (PTSD) allows people to quickly communicate behavior and possible past experiences.

Symptoms, then, become a way that private experiences can enter the public, as flashbacks and jitteriness can be witnessed by and discussed with others. Trade-offs between personal and collective responses lead to a negotiation of silence and speech—when and what do survivors communicate and when are they silenced versus silent.

What many survivors, laypeople, and even clinicians don't always consider is the sociomoral dimension of PTSD: the moral injury and shift in social identity that changes how survivors perceive their roles in a society that doesn't understand or acknowledge their experiences.

Inherent in the term *trauma* is the idea of moral injustice or a failing of society to uphold and protect. We are all aware of cultures that fail their members—think of toxic masculinity, the stoicism of the military, the self-sacrifice of physicians. These environments make people hold in and keep private the wrongs they've experienced. In fact, these cultures often teach people that they have to stay silent to survive in them. Healing, then, is an individual experience, though the cause of the injury is not.

Silence is often required for survival, but it comes at the cost of historical memory and effecting change. Using the term *PTSD* provides a way for people to express that something has happened to them. Holding memories in their bodies, themselves, and their societies can move them through a process of resistance and repair.

Many survivors of campus sexual assault end up with significantly lower GPAs, increased likelihood of dropping out or withdrawing, and problems with learning. But Gabriela felt emboldened to speak out, mainly to help support other survivors that she knew were also suffering in silence. Confronting what happened to her during the assault as well as facing the aftermath allowed her to create a narrative that reshaped the memory from trauma. She created a new story of resilience and resistance.

Memories of the assault's wounds left her with a humiliated self-image. In my office, through the process of healing, Gabriela shifts from internalizing shame and self-blame to recognizing that the true responsibility lies with the assailant and the societal systems that enabled her harm.

By moving the burden from her individual self outward to society, she moves from a place where she feels broken and incapable of coping to one where she sees the culture itself as broken and in need of change. This shift empowers her, transforming her narrative from one of victimhood and defeat to one of resistance and strength.

While the dangers that we've experienced in the past can shatter our lives into fragments, we have the power to piece them together into a new form. The aftermath of trauma casts synaptic shadows on our inner lives, but by shining the light of conscious awareness on those hidden spaces, we can change the story. The narratives we tell about our lives can change.

This doesn't mean nothing is real. Rather, our *interpretation* of reality is always a work in progress. Memory is about perspective. The stories we remember are part truth, part meaning, and part connection. The more we understand that, the more compassion we can bring to ourselves and to the way others remember too.

So, what we remember is very much influenced by the events we're remembering, the situations we're in, and who we are sharing with. But there's even more to the story. Our memories are also shaped by unconscious forces that set up repeated patterns of instability in a desperate attempt to make us rewrite that which we could not resolve.

Action Tools for Memories

A. Reconstruct with Curiosity, Not Certainty

1. Be flexible in the autobiography of your memories. The brain organizes memories into mental templates that help simplify and store experiences. Over time, you shape your identity through these storylines, even if the details shift. Notice the patterns in the stories you repeat about your past. Do the stories still serve you? Are they helping you grow or are they keeping you stuck?

2. Treat your memory like a live document. Neuroscience shows that memory isn't a fixed recording; it's a reconstruction built by your brain. Every time you retrieve a memory, you're also rewriting it. Revisit important memories with the mindset of an editor. Ask yourself, *What might have changed in how I see this?* You're not losing the truth; you're layering in perspective. Accepting memory's limitations boosts psychological flexibility, reduces defensiveness in relationships, and creates space for empathy and dialogue.

3. Use emotion as a clue, not a conclusion. Emotion strengthens memory encoding but can also distort it. The amygdala flags emotional moments as important, but that doesn't mean the memories are accurate. Provide context to intensely vivid memories—what emotions might be amplifying those memories?

B. Allow Your Memory to Evolve

4. Treat gaps with gentle curiosity. The brain often fills in blanks, generating memory fragments that make sense, even if they aren't true. This is adaptive, not deceptive. If parts of your past are a blur, don't rush to fill them with certainty. Gaps can point to stress, trauma, or simply moments that didn't register as significant. Instead of forcing recall, try guided reflection: *What else was happening in my life then? Who might remember this differently?* Forgetting may be your brain's way of protecting you.

5. Shift the goal from proving to validating. Instead of pressuring yourself to recover crystal-clear memories, focus on validating your current emotional experience. You will likely never know all the facts of what happened in the past, so instead, focus on how you feel when you think of that time. Your body stores information, even if you don't have details.

C. Reach for Connection over Correction

6. Share to remember and question what you adopt. Social remembering helps you fill in the blanks, but it also subtly rewires your memories. Conversations with others can strengthen, alter, or even rewrite our memories. When you're sharing old stories with friends or family, ask what they remember about it. Compare narratives without rushing to merge them, and treat differences as informative. Holding multiple versions helps you understand not just the event but what it meant to each person.

7. Shift focus to collective healing and repair. If you've lived through a traumatic violation, shift the burden of individual healing toward societal responsibility. Ask: *What kind of culture allowed this to happen?* Healing accelerates when we recognize that pain isn't always solely personal; it's often political, relational, and structural.

3

Our Life in Cycles: Repeating What We Could Not Resolve

As I sat under a tattered mosquito net hiding from former child soldiers in Bujumbura, Burundi, I asked myself, *How did I end up here?* In a form of trauma reenactment, I had re-created a scene of danger, one in which I felt helpless and shocked—much as I had felt when my father was assaulted and kidnapped.

Today, as someone who recognizes the ways in which unaddressed trauma can pilot behavior unconsciously, I can see that it wasn't only altruism that led me to unflinchingly and repeatedly expose myself to dangerous situations. Yet it was only after I had truly been threatened—and experienced paralyzing terror—that I began to uncover the deeper pull of wanting to confront a violent death.

I now recognize that my decisions were my way of trying to achieve mastery over the instability and paralyzing hopelessness I had felt after my father's assault. The technical term for this is *repetition compulsion,* and its job is to make a person unconsciously repeat a similar trauma of the past. I had unconsciously re-created a danger similar to my father's. My unconscious must have believed that this time around, I would be able to control the outcome.

In the face of my own trauma, I leaned into my version of stability, re-creating that which I was familiar with. Paradoxically, repeating the past created more instability. States of uncertainty *became* my stability, integrated into who I knew myself to be—my values, beliefs, purpose, and coping in life.

Maps of the Past

More often than one would think, the instability in our lives is caused by our making the same poor decisions through reconstructions of the past. We reenact scenarios from long ago, hoping for better outcomes. Control and mastery seem within our grasp, but despite our best intentions, we find ourselves in the same mess we thought we'd left behind.

But why would people want to relive some of the most painful parts of their lives, such as being raised by an overly critical mother or an alcoholic father? Times of exploitation, violation, abandonment, and neglect are all aspects of life that people desperately want to forget—not re-create.

Social modeling plays a role, as you develop patterns through watching how others behave: What you see is how you act. Yet contrary to popular belief, it's not only your relational environment that shapes you. Repeating the past is hardwired in the human brain and nervous system. Neuroscience shows that early life experiences are embedded deep in the brain, affecting not only emotional memories but also neuronal synapses that shape learning, perception, and behavior.

The brain develops in relation to early life experiences, embedding both implicit and explicit memories that help you learn how to behave in a particular way or seek out people who seem familiar, effectively re-creating the emotional environment of childhood and your behavioral response.

Imagine a map of interweaving roads formed by relational memories and adaptive behaviors. The main destination: psychological survival. As a child, you explored your physical body and social and personal relationships and figured out how all of that was related to your inner feelings.

So you tried things out. When a bully harassed you, maybe you fought back or maybe you hid. If your grandmother was disparaging, perhaps you learned to appease her by your accomplishments. You found you could gain the attention of your distant father by standing out in some way—by being the jokester, graduating at the top of your class, or getting in trouble at school.

As you tried out different ways of responding to the world around you, you found behaviors that helped you cope at the time: withdrawal, overachieving, hiding, acting out, placating. All of these likely worked for you back then, but at a cost: awareness.

The more routine and habitual your behavior is, the less aware you are of doing it. Maybe you say "I'm sorry" for actions that have nothing to do with you; maybe you challenge another's opinion even when that person is agreeing with you; maybe you are drawn to someone who elicits the same behaviors that you want to squash. All of this happens without a supervising mind made of the inner adult wisdom you've gained over the years.

Throughout my clinical practice, I've worked with the conscious narratives that patients come in with—the grocery list of stressors they want to talk about. I hear stories about how a partner wronged them and explanations to validate why they had to stop talking to a parent or why they engage in passive-aggressive behaviors with the boss.

But I also try to uncover the subconscious memories that fuel the stories and explanations: the last argument over dishes left undone that prompted a divorce, being excluded from a conversation at a holiday dinner that motivated one to stop talking to the family for two years.

And I attend to the deeper, more hidden, and often more powerful influences that drive behavior. Repetition compulsion—reenactments of past traumas—are powerful and insidious motivators that place people in situations where danger is likely to happen (myself in Burundi); make them gravitate toward harmful relationships (such as the woman who swore she'd never marry an alcoholic like her father and was surprised when her husband developed a sex addiction); or lead them to repeat painful situations of the past (like a man who'd grown up feeling invisible in a chaotic family and as an adult instinctively withdrew from emotional intimacy in his marriage, creating a similar loneliness).

While people believe they can gain control over their past instabilities or traumas by reexperiencing them, the unconscious process of repetition compulsion actually does the opposite by creating more suffering and intensifying a sense of confusion and helplessness at not being able to master the situation.

The well-trodden path is reinforced repeatedly. People who have experienced adversity often continue to make the same lamentable decisions when they reenact scenarios from the past; they are hoping for better outcomes and are confused and disappointed when they find themselves in instability yet again.

"I Know It's Not Right, but I Just Can't Stop Myself"

Three years ago, Amanda, a high-performing political lobbyist, had little time for a relationship. After getting stuck in one unsatisfying relationship after another with workaholic men who had little time for her, she gave up on dating and focused solely on her career. That is, until she met Ryan. She bumped into him at a coffee shop and was captivated by his gentle demeanor and the ease with which he carried himself. Radiating a sense of calm, Ryan appeared to be the perfect match for Amanda's near-constant frenzy.

Amanda became enamored of Ryan's earnestness. He was youthful, hardworking, and charming. Values merged as they shared their dreams and daily lives together. Two years later, the couple got engaged, and Amanda became preoccupied with wedding planning— but out of necessity, not desire. Party planning was tedious. Ryan had little interest in the process, so Amanda took it on herself to orchestrate the nuptials.

Soon, Amanda noticed a fundamental problem: She didn't feel prioritized by Ryan. Ten-minute conversations between dinner and his return to work became the default in their daily lives. Since meetings and tasks were constant, Ryan had little energy to connect with her. There was no way of spontaneously sharing emotional depth, let alone moments of joy.

Resentment and apathy quickly grew. Ryan unpredictably and inexplicably had long nights at work; he became frustrated with Amanda over how unkempt the house was and complained about her "nagging" to connect.

Four months before their wedding, Amanda comes to see me, feeling stuck, dissatisfaction growing. Initially, she says, she couldn't imagine life without him, but now she struggles to imagine a future with him. Trapped with an emotionally distant fiancé, she is desperate for some kind of magic—a different way of communicating or behaving that will help them be more united.

Feeling held back and undervalued, Amanda isn't sure what to do. She says that their arguments often devolved into hostility, with Ryan telling her that not only were her ideas stupid, but she was as well. His near-constant remarks about how controlling she is confuse Amanda, as she thinks the opposite. She often asks Ryan for his input, only to be met with disdain.

If Ryan were constantly disrespectful, Amanda might have been able to leave him then and there. But the relationship is toxic because he has moments of charm. His intermittent adoration keeps jolting her back to the relationship she pines for. Vacillating between a pull to save what was and a push to end it, she's lost trust in herself: "How did this happen? How did I end up in this?" she cries.

On the heels of this, Amanda assures me—and herself—that Ryan is a catch. "He's sweet," she says. Focusing on how adoring he was during their first six months and on his potential as a good father, Amanda tries to brush aside present concerns.

Loved ones have already booked flights for the wedding. Caterer, venue, and florist plans have evolved. Amanda is stuck in a sunk-cost fallacy: She and her loved ones have already invested so much time, money, and effort in this relationship that she believes she has to continue, even if doing so may cause her more harm than benefit. She tells herself that conflict might strengthen their bond, and she feels personally responsible for spearheading a resilient marriage.

So she focuses on making Ryan's life easier: She reminds him to run every morning, schedules his doctor's appointments, and calls his family on his behalf. Amanda even stops by his office with a packed lunch to make sure he has healthy meals. Once when she was there, she canceled her own meetings to help him organize his files and desk.

We're often taught to be flexible, understanding, and compassionate with our partners, as "no one's perfect." Happy romantic relationships are portrayed as lasting for decades without major arguments, so people feel they should move beyond the other's hurtful comments or behaviors: "That's just the way they are," they say and then change the subject. There are, of course, clear advantages to distraction and avoidance: They keep the peace. At least in the short term.

Amanda is consumed with a gnawing inner turmoil that she can't resolve. "Dr. Song, I don't know how I got here. If I'm really honest with myself, I know it's not right, but I just can't stop myself."

These words are at the heart of repetition compulsion. Trapped in a stable ambiguity, she obsesses over the same question: Should I stay or should I go?

Reconditioning the Brain

Ann Graybiel and researchers at the Massachusetts Institute of Technology sought to understand how habits form in the brain. They trained rats to navigate a T-shaped maze using a sound cue to signal whether to turn left or right. When the rats made the correct turn, they received a treat—either chocolate milk or sugar water.

Eventually, the researchers removed the rewards, but the rats still followed the sound cues and made the correct turns. Later, the rewards were reintroduced—but this time, the chocolate milk was laced with a substance that made the rats feel sick. Even after learning to avoid drinking it, the rats still ran to the chocolate milk side of the maze when cued.

The study reveals something powerful: once a behavior becomes automatic, it can override even negative consequences. The human unconscious mind isn't all that different. People have an instinctive bias for maintaining the familiar and avoiding the new, even when the former is harmful.

The researchers found a "deliberation circuit" in the brain that's active when you're making decisions and a "habit circuit" when you're on autopilot. Although your actions may seem automatic, it turns out that behaviors are under the control of circuits in your cortex that supervise moment-to-moment moves.

This is good news. It means we can redraw the map with new behaviors, language, and relational experiences to grow and stimulate new patterns. Self-reflection with an engaged, empathetic, and non-judgmental listener who can astutely notice patterns and identify conflicts can empower you to attend to your actions. When you're aware of the larger picture, you can consciously choose your path.

Patients come to my office to start or stop medications, explore past experiences, or focus on current dilemmas around rumination or despair, but regardless of what brings them in, a large percentage of my patients suffer from a common phenomenon: They are repeating past traumas that were not resolved.

While many assume that repetition compulsion only shows up in personal or romantic relationships, I've seen it emerge just as often in professional settings—like finding yourself stuck in a hostile work environment or repeatedly feeling dismissed or undervalued by someone in a position of power. These patterns often trace back to earlier emotional injuries that were never fully understood or healed.

Over the years, I've developed a framework for exploring patterns that underlie daily instabilities. For ease, the framework can be remembered by the acronym REPEAT, and I've found the process helpful in assessing and breaking a tenacious cycle of reenacting.

R *Is for* Recognize the Underlying Problem

I have a suspicion that there is a reenactment at play with Amanda, so I want to explore what the true problem is.

Amanda is certain the problem is Ryan. "He's too passive. If he would just find some friends or switch jobs to one he actually enjoys, we'd be fine." She drafts lists in her head: podcasts he should listen to, books he should read, ways to structure his week. It passes as generous and even loving. And also keeps her where she's most comfortable: as the competent, calm one calling the shots.

When Ryan shrugs or stalls, Amanda logs it as proof that she's the only one doing the work. She pushes solutions; he goes quiet, so she presses harder. What she wants is relief—more closeness, more steadiness—but it comes out as instruction that he hears as judgment.

Tension started creeping in and moments of irritation replaced some of the early spark. But she chalked it up to what she believed was the fate of any long-term relationship—*no couple stays in the honeymoon phase forever*, she thought. Frustrations were seen as a part of settling in.

As soon as Amanda hears her own words, she tries to backtrack: "Ryan is a really sweet guy; he is just stunted. If he would go to therapy, I think we'd be fine," she offers. I smile at how earnest and caring she is. And how much work we have to do.

Continuing to turn to loved ones for attunement, validation, and attention that they have repeatedly shown they are unable to provide only leads to more pain. So much suffering could be avoided if we could accept the reality that some people cannot be who we need them to be.

Amanda is falling into a trap that many of us do—she's trying to solve the wrong problem. Fixating on Ryan only perpetuates arguments, which increases Amanda's despair and the distance between them. Focusing on the problem of an unsatisfying engagement may provide clarity in the short term, but it will lead to more resentment, as Ryan becomes frustrated with someone trying to change him, or to another reenactment cycle in Amanda's next relationship. I'm sensing there's more to Amanda's suffering than just a man who refuses to go to therapy.

E *Is for* Explore the Repetition

"He's emotionally stunted. I don't know that I can grow with him," she laments.

"Yet here you are with him," I state. "What draws you to him?"

"When he's not stressed, we have moments of fun together. He feels like my person—my home."

Often when people aren't aware they're being pulled by the undertow of a reenactment, they feel the partner is reminiscent of "home," even when that home was unsafe for them.

"How does being with someone emotionally stunted remind you of home?" I'm merely trying to understand how she learned this was normal.

As a child, Amanda navigated chaos by retreating into a closet lined with string lights and soft pillows, a small sanctuary from the volatility downstairs. Her father's presence was predictably unpredictable—sometimes he was a source of fear, other times of delight, spinning her wildly on the beach. Through an emotional whiplash of affection laced with blame, love tangled with manipulation. She absorbed a lesson early on that's hard to unlearn: The difference between comfort and harm is hard to recognize when both come from the same source.

In the absence of a dedicated caretaker, at age twelve, she stepped into the role of the adult. Responsibility became her refuge, achievement her coping mechanism. She was busy holding everything together, but no one was holding her. Amanda's needs went unnoticed by others, and eventually she lost track of them herself. Now that she's an adult, the relational dynamics that once exhausted her also feel strangely familiar. Not because they're healthy but because they're *home.*

Amanda recognizes her reenactment. Desperately wanting—needing—her partner to be more emotionally responsive, to give her more attention or adore her, she over-functions in an attempt to make yet another man prove that she's worthy. In a short time, she's re-created the same situation of emotional isolation, over-functioning, and desperation to be seen.

Amanda's underlying problem isn't only Ryan; it's also how to manage the aftereffects of growing up with an emotionally unavailable parent who had a serious alcohol addiction. She begins to understand that her repetition is an attempt to seek mastery over chaos and validation that she's lovable. She partners up with oppressive men to prove she can change another person through her love and redemption.

P *Is for* Pause the Pattern

Amanda internalized the belief that she deserved mistreatment. Desperate to gain the love and acceptance of a man, especially one who was emotionally distant, physically unavailable, and dismissive, Amanda found ways to cope with her father's abuse. Emotional malnourishment was familiar.

If you're stuck in a trap of suffering, awareness of the reenactment can help you intentionally move toward a less destructive path. But I've found something unsettling: Even when people are aware that a repetition is causing them pain, like the rats in the maze, they still continue turning toward it.

After discovering the link between past and present pain, many people want to move forward—and quickly. There's the spark of insight—*Yes! Now I see!*—and they feel they've "dealt" with the issue. They believe that recognizing the reenactment ends the cycle, so their efforts to change the status quo stop here. But there's more work to do, and sadly, there's no shortcut.

Over the next few weeks, Amanda tells her best friends, sister, college girlfriends, and anyone else who seems interested all about her compulsion to repeat the past. Sharing insight is powerful, but it can also be limiting. Talking at length about why she's drawn to Ryan is like playing the same song over and over again—it's still the same song. She needs to write new lyrics.

Intellectual understanding should be followed by a pause. I help Amanda embark on a practice to cultivate curiosity through self-compassion. When Amanda has an argument with Ryan, her first response has been to attack herself. Now aware that she is ensnared in an unhealthy, familiar pattern, she then chastises herself for becoming entangled with someone like him and for not having the courage to leave.

Recognizing the pattern helps, but on its own it doesn't create change. To truly shift the pattern, she has to turn toward the vulnerable emotions that are stirred up—for example, the shame of being caught in the very situation she thought she'd grown past.

I guide her to pause there, not rush past the shame or numb it with action but to sit with it long enough to see it differently. This does not need to be the end of her story. The repetition may have reappeared, but that doesn't make her progress meaningless—there's still room to pivot, choose something new, and recognize that being aware *while still in the pattern* is actually a step forward.

This is where I invite her to hold a tension that many struggle with—especially in a culture steeped in the myth of redemptive suffering with pain transformed to triumph, where what doesn't kill you makes you stronger, where the underdog rises. But there's a quiet harm to that expectation when it serves as an emotional yardstick: If you're not stronger yet, are you failing?

So when Amanda's feeling down on herself about where she is in life, I encourage her to refuse to let this moment be the period at the end of a story she didn't choose. We make space for quiet forms of strength: choosing not to reenact the past, setting a boundary, grieving what never was, and living with self-compassion. A pause creates space to face hard emotions and rewrite not just the story—but where she thinks it ends.

E *Is for* Embrace

You need to experience the feelings associated with an emotional wound in order to neutralize the power it has on future behaviors.

As a child, Amanda struggled with feeling unseen, alone, resentful, and responsible for her father's well-being. Too young to have the skills or awareness to manage, she pushed these feelings aside and found her own form of survival through accomplishment, compliance, and nurturing others. These coping skills worked—until they didn't. Now that she is an adult, her childhood emotions and adaptive responses are motivating forces in choosing her life partner.

Even when we rationally decide to change, lingering emotions keep us stuck. Unless we actively confront the heavy emotions, we're still bound to them. One way to manage an emotion is to intentionally activate an opposing one. I ask Amanda to recall a hurtful memory of her father and then imagine a scenario in which she feels comforted. "It can be as fantastical as you want—talking lions on clouds or angels flying around, whatever you need to create a haven of ultimate protection, safety, unconditional love, and nurturing."

Over the next twenty minutes, she rewrites her story to include a garden of puppies that are constantly by her side. I ask, "What else would you need to feel absolutely unburdened, loved, and nurtured?" She brings in a loving fairy godmother who flies around her as she runs across the lush grass, ensuring her safety. While she probably doesn't notice this, I can see her shoulders drop with ease as her breath deepens.

Amanda has learned to release the power certain emotions have on her by recalling her imagined safe haven whenever she feels them. No longer flung around mindlessly by her feelings, she has learned to respond to them, not just react. I've seen time and time again how this simple practice of pausing, embracing, and working with emotions gives a sense of competence, self-efficacy, and, ultimately, healing.

A *Is for* Act with Intention

Amanda is now ready to move forward. After practicing embracing her emotions and letting them pass through her instead of blocking them or distracting herself from them, she learns that those difficult feelings of hopelessness and fear no longer have to control her. Now she can begin to set an intention for a preferred future.

Strategizing a detailed plan of action can be time-consuming and draining and leave you wallowing in stable ambiguity. But thinking of a current instability as a stepping-stone on the path toward a brighter future can move you from paralysis to action. Surprisingly, research shows that visualizing an outcome is five times more effective than just thinking about a goal. So I ask Amanda what she wants her life to look like. How does she want to feel in a relationship?

"Well, I want to feel loved, but honestly, I don't think anyone will love me. I want to feel competent at communicating and managing conflict, but I don't think I can do that." She looks at the floor, ashamed. Unfortunately, this is often a by-product of chronic emotional injury: shame, insecurity, and a sense of being unlovable.

Amanda has high relational capacity, especially if she's able to manage her compulsion to repeat the past, so I help her remember the skills and experiences in which she's been successful. She reminisces about people and events in her past—an aunt who always made her feel loved; a recent argument with her best friend during which she was able to listen and effectively respond to how she'd inadvertently hurt her.

To ground the visualization, I ask her to call on her senses with each memory: Was there a certain perfume that her aunt wore? Did she see her friend relax after their relational repair? Amanda now has actions she can take, a guide that counters her belief that she is not lovable and not competent in resolving conflict. She can visualize how she wants to feel. Which leads us to the next issue: Will she join Ryan at the altar next month or not?

T *Is for* Think Through the Maze

Amanda ruminates about everything and nothing at the same time, mostly asking herself, *What should I do?*, but without coming up with any meaningful solutions. In her quietest moments, she finds a few minutes of true connection—to herself. "I was sitting on the couch one night when Ryan was out, and I thought, *I can't look at myself in the mirror anymore.* I'm losing respect for myself and don't even know who I am," she tells me.

Amanda has made an important discovery and begun the process of internalizing a new identity. These repetitive patterns exist because they feel familiar. If you see yourself as someone who always over-functions in relationships, then you're likely to keep doing it, even when it hurts.

To break these patterns, you need to build new narratives beyond your behavior toward who you are becoming. Studies on identity-based motivation show that people are far more likely to change their habits when those changes align with their desired identities. The next time you're unsure about what to do, try asking yourself, *Would someone like me do something like that?* It's a simple way to tune into your inner compass and align your actions with who you're becoming. If you shift your identity from "I over-function in relationships" to "I'm someone who sets boundaries," the behavior starts to follow.

I encourage Amanda to ask herself, *Who am I becoming?* She surprises herself with clarity: "I want to be someone who acts with self-respect," she responds, straightening her spine with a confidence I haven't really seen before.

Amanda went on to pave a new path forward. She postponed the wedding out of clarity, not fear, by choosing strength over self-sacrifice. She asked better questions: *Am I hoping he'll change, or am I changing what I expect from love?* Every time she felt devalued and ignored, she paused, reflected, and chose a path aligned with her values, not her past. She and Ryan did eventually break up, and she felt she did more than just end a relationship; she ended a lifelong pattern.

It's commonly believed that repetition compulsion is fully negative. But I've been impressed by people like Amanda, those who have shown that reenactments can serve as a path to understanding and healing. Those who are able to embrace the instability in their lives are often able to confront their repeated pasts, using repetition compulsion to their advantage and creating new paths that free them from old hurts.

Action Tools for Our Life in Cycles

1. Recognize the underlying problem. You can't change what you can't name. Patterns repeat because they're familiar, but they aren't always good. Awareness is the first disruption. Write down difficult relational or work moments that feel familiar and ask yourself if there's an emotional echo at play. Try a pattern journal to document triggers, reactions, and emotional responses.

2. Explore the repetition. Most dysfunctional patterns started off as strategies for survival, with repetition a form of adaptation. Understanding the origin story can turn confusion into clarity. Reflect on where you learned your pattern of behavior. Ask *When did I learn this was normal?*

3. Pause the pattern. Self-judgment keeps you stuck, but curiosity can move you forward. Instead of reacting to your situation with guilt or shame, approach your triggers like a researcher—with curiosity. Ask *What am I needing right now?* Acknowledge the pain of being in the cycle, then move the timestamp of the ending, recognizing the story doesn't stop here but continues through the work being done.

4. Embrace the emotion. Reenactments are fueled by undigested past emotions that linger. When you were a child with limited forms of coping, you managed difficult emotions as best you could. By bringing those emotions to the forefront, you can shift the pattern from unconscious to conscious awareness. Honor the pain of not receiving the safety, consistency, and validation that you should have. Create your imagined sanctuary to self-soothe when the difficult emotions emerge.

5. Act with intention. Create an intention of how you want to feel. Visualize yourself attaining this and call on all your senses. Ask *How do I want to feel?* Imagine yourself in a situation where you feel this way—what do you see, smell, hear, and feel around you?

6. Think through the maze. Change lasts when it's about who you are, not just what you do. Ask *Would someone like me do something like that?* Tap into your inner compass or internalize a new identity by asking yourself not *What should I do?* but *Who am I becoming?*

PART II

RITUALS

Bamboo (대나무, *daenamu*, in Korean; 竹, *zhú*, in Chinese; 竹, *take*, in Japanese): One of the fastest-growing plants in the world, versatile, with remarkable strength, bamboo is able to survive the harshest winter and send up shoots again in the spring. In Asian art, bamboo symbolizes tenacity, humility, receptivity, and integrity.

On March 6, 2018, I was having a lot of trouble focusing on work, and I wasn't sure why. This wasn't an altogether rare occurrence, as I was working full-time and parenting two kids under the age of two. This particular inability to focus, though, felt different. It was hard to read, and I was distracted when I was with my patients. Instead of proper meals, I relied on cereal. Exhausted, I had had vivid dreams the previous night that I could not remember. I was able to accomplish the bare minimum needed for the day but I did so with an undercurrent of terror and listlessness.

That evening, as I spooned up some more cereal, it occurred to me that the difficulty focusing, poor sleep, and buzzing unease were actually the norm for this day: It was the anniversary of my father's death. One would think that after twenty-four years, I'd be better prepared to manage the grief. Every year on this day, guilt creeps in that I'm not doing more to honor his life. Yet what surprises me is the anxiety I feel about my own mortality. My father's death anniversary always hits me with instability, as it calls me to attend to feelings about death that aren't usually on my agenda.

For years, I tried to avoid reminders of his death. If I avoided thinking about my father, I rationalized, my yearning and sadness would eventually dissolve. I could continue to go about my days fully in charge of when, where, and with whom I shared my memories of him. This worked, more or less, until my second child was born. At this point, my erratic grief was coupled with deep sadness and a shaking sense of fear at the thought of dying in my forties like my father—and missing out on seeing my children grow.

I know I'm not alone in practicing avoidance of anything to do with death, as recognition of one's own mortality registers as a threat in a specific area of the brain. Naturally, people resist thinking about their own deaths or that of loved ones. The path of least resistance is to avoid.

With a newborn and a toddler to care for, I searched for a path to guide me through this anniversary day. My grieving felt unfinished at best and ignored at worst. I turned to my Korean heritage for inspiration. During summer visits to my grandparents' home in Seoul, I remember watching my aunts bumping into each other in a crowded kitchen as they prepared soup and fish while my grandfather burned incense in a *jesa* ceremony that honored deceased family members as far back as five generations.

Honoring the dead, especially one's ancestors, is an important part of Korean culture, tied to Confucius's teachings of piety and love for one's family. Many Koreans believe that after someone dies, the spirit doesn't immediately leave Earth but stays with surviving family members for multiple generations. The *jesa* tradition celebrates and honors deceased family members to show respect, strengthen the bond between the living family and the deceased, and encourage the deceased spirit to watch over living descendants.

Now, every March 6, I engage in my own personal *jesa*. I prepare an altar: a black mother-of-pearl table adorned with stacked oranges and apples (symbolizing good health for loved ones), layered rice cakes (for celebration), and a bowl of dumpling soup (for long life). I give ten ceremonial bows in front of a photo of my father to show respect and love. Then, while sipping a cup of his favorite black Lipton tea, I reminisce about going hiking with him and watching him groom our dog, and I think about the ways in which I'm grateful for his presence in my life.

Engaging in this ritual every year doesn't prevent the ache of guilt I feel around his anniversary, but it does allow me to feel more in control and to focus my emotions. My jitteriness eases, and guilt subsides. I find comfort in the process. Physical stiffness and aches abate as I heal the internal knots on his death anniversary. A fresh sense of agency circulates through me as I intentionally embrace his death as well as his life. I feel deeply connected to him while also imagining a satisfying future without him.

What's powerful for me in the *jesa* ritual is that it's more than just a memorial ceremony for the deceased. The ritual is a scaffold for my pain and connects me to ancestors and culture past and present, all of which increases my capacity to embrace the intensely emotional and disruptive grieving that comes with memories of how my father lived and died.

My narratives create a world with an inherent set of values and beliefs that form the content of my ritual that I imbue with meaning and use to connect with something outside myself. Rituals, for me, go beyond actions. They are an act of communication.

Rituals are reflections of the values, fears, and hopes that shape individuals and societies. In many cases, the power of ritual lies not in what is said but in what is felt. Not all emotions and experiences need to be processed verbally. Sometimes words just get in the way. Leaning on rituals through the processes of separation, liminality, and reintegration helps us find motivation amid the turmoil, create movement in stuckness, and turn doubts into strength.

4

Separation and Loss: Honoring What Was

People who have gone through really hard times often talk about the positives—how they learned to be resourceful when their parents neglected them, strong-willed in the face of a bully who targeted them, or confident and self-assured after a dysfunctional relationship. I probably did the same thing, trying to find the silver lining to make the hardships meaningful and worth something. But now that I've explored more, I'm not sure the suffering was worth it.

Old friends and family members who knew me in my teenage years often make a connection to my present way of coping: "You've always been so steady," they'll say, or "You've been so responsible and caretaking ever since your father died."

Whether or not I agree with that, it is true that I responded to hardships in my early life by over-functioning. I doggedly tried to keep everything under control to get me back to equilibrium. Homework was completed right after school, laundry was folded, and dinner was made. Friends who were suffering the pangs of unrequited love, despairing after a failed exam, or laid low at home with the flu for a week knew that I would be there for them.

For some people, myself included, coping by over-functioning has been a curse disguised as a blessing, especially as I age. Reflexively, I take responsibility for others' well-being and manage situations that aren't mine to handle. Being hyper-competent helps me control a flurry of emotions, especially in a culture that praises efficiency.

At one point, though, physical exhaustion and emotional depletion led to resentment, unrealistic expectations of myself, and an imbalance of reciprocity in relationships. I've often heard armchair therapists talk about the need to "process one's loss." What, exactly, does that mean?

For me, processing the separation and loss from my father's death meant respecting a numbing fear that fragmented my memories, uncovering the unspoken narratives that controlled my life outlook, and managing the urge to cope in ways that might have worked in the past but now had limitations.

While I have worked hard at rewriting my narratives with more control and directive, I'd be the first to acknowledge that some ways of coping haven't meaningfully changed with time. This is where rituals come in—they build on and supplement narratives.

Separation and loss are universal experiences, yet each person's loss is individual. Everyone who comes through my office door is influenced by a loss: the executive who was let go from her job, the child whose parents are getting divorced, the pregnant woman who struggles with the identity changes of new motherhood, the refugee newcomer who has lost his place of belonging.

Loss is a destabilizing force. Whether it's real or perceived, experienced or threatened, expected or desired, losses shake your sense of security and threaten your identity. When you lose a loved one, your sense of community and relationships are made vulnerable. Losing a job, house, or material wealth can all jeopardize your sense of security, safety, culture, identity, and status. Separating creates a sense of instability that leaves you wondering how to move forward.

For some, loss paralyzes and silences; for others, it motivates with newfound creativity. Even if the loss was expected, the emotions are rarely easily defined.

During times of instability when there's no clear and easy solution to the problems in front of us, we can lean on rituals to provide structure and a sense of control.

Around the world, people turn to rituals in the face of loss: they wear black after the death of loved ones; delete all photos and messages after a breakup; shake hands with the opposing team after losing a game. Yet there's nothing uniform about grieving practices. Egyptian women are supposed to wail throughout a funeral to prove the value of the deceased, whereas in Bali, crying at funerals is seen as shameful. Jewish law dictates coffins should be wooden and plain, whereas in the Greater Accra Region of Ghana, fantasy coffins—caskets shaped like airplanes or Coke bottles—help celebrate the deceased.

Beyond Magic

At this very moment in every part of the world, people are engaging in rituals. Often seen as a rigid set of superstitious or magical behaviors, rituals are commonly thought to be used solely by faith healers and New Age spiritualists.

But rituals aren't only for those inclined to the supernatural or spiritual. You almost certainly engage in many rituals without knowing that you're doing so. There are major rituals of transformation and transition—baptisms, bar mitzvahs, graduations, marriages, and funerals—but everyone also engages in daily rituals to decrease anxiety, perform better, and improve social bonding.

Psychologists generally define a ritual as a "predefined sequence of symbolic actions often characterized by formality and repetition that lacks direct instrumental purpose." They convince the brain of predictability and constancy in the face of uncertainty. The most meaningful traditions and cultural practices in religion, politics, business, education, sports, and the military teach participants about where they come from and provide an immediate sense of connection.

Across history and cultures, family dinners, holiday traditions, and the passing down of heirlooms are rituals woven into the social fabric. Deep bows in a monastery signal respect, modesty, and a physical expression of Buddha's teachings; wearing what they believe are lucky underpants during a game gives athletes the confidence of positive thinking; and covering mirrors during a Jewish shiva reminds mourners to concentrate on the deceased.

These shared practices aren't just cultural decorations; they create an invisible scaffolding to support people through life's ups and downs. Instability is woven into the human experience. What's fascinating is how rituals can prepare us for navigating instability. At every moment, people are scanning their surroundings, measuring their ability to cope, and adjusting their actions accordingly. People create rituals to give themselves a sense of control over what they cannot predict.

A collective rehearsal of sorts, rituals are like fire drills—you learn what to do before facing an actual fire. They allow you to prepare for the inevitable instability to come. Communities with robust shared rituals have greater resilience during natural disasters than those without, suggesting that these practiced patterns of togetherness create psychological resources people can draw upon when the ground beneath them shifts.

In an increasingly unpredictable world of climate change, technological disruptions, and pandemic threats, these seemingly simple acts of coming together in structured ways become more than comforting traditions. They become essential training grounds. Rituals aren't just habits; they are a way of imposing order on chaos, transforming the unknown into something manageable, even if only in our minds.

But how do rituals provide control and predictability in an otherwise chaotic world? If blowing out candles on a birthday cake, tossing coins into fountains, or crossing fingers for good luck were truly meaningless, we would have stopped doing them centuries ago. But they endure. So what kind of sorcery do rituals hold?

Turns out, it's less about sorcery and more about science. Rituals do more than help people find control. Studies show that they can ease anxiety in almost any high-pressure endeavor—even if the ritual is painful.

On a small island in Mauritius, off the eastern coast of Madagascar, a Hindu community celebrates a ten-day Thimithi festival with fasting, prayers, and body piercings done with needles through the tongue and forehead and two-centimeter-long skewers through the cheeks. After this, a procession heads for the temple, the participants walking barefoot on the burning asphalt in the sun for several hours without food or water while performing rituals to ward off evil spirits.

If you haven't fainted already, there's more. Thimithi culminates in a fire-walking ritual. Once the fire-walkers reach the temple, they proceed over the edges of swords and finish by walking across a bed of glowing charcoal.

Psychologist Ronald Fischer and his team compared the changes in levels of happiness, fatigue, and heart rate pre- and post-ritual of three groups: fire-walkers, their families, and unrelated spectators. If someone told me to walk barefoot over asphalt for long distances without food or water and end by walking across a bed of coals, I would swiftly decline, but the researchers found that post-ritual, the fire-walkers reported higher levels of happiness than the other two groups (their families reported the highest levels of fatigue). For this community, engaging in these rituals that involved pain, injury, or trauma held some kind of psychological benefit.

Why? Perhaps it's because losing oneself doesn't always lead to misery. Free-falling into something larger than oneself can bring intense happiness. Social scientists call this *collective effervescence*, a shared emotional experience that binds communities together. The benefits of transcendence, including walking on fire, extend beyond the individual.

This is the power of rituals. They bridge the gap between life and death, memory and experience, aloneness and connection. Forcing your mind to focus on something concrete and actionable brings you one step closer to the ideal world in which you want to live. Through ritual, we connect to an aspect of existence that we cannot see—hopes, dreams, and intentions—especially for those experiencing an unwelcome separation or loss.

Grieving Loss and the Luck of the Draw

As many people who have experienced the loss of a loved one know, having a well-trodden path to structure one's grief (the feeling after loss) and mourning (the processing of grief) can be comforting. Having to rely on one's own way of coping makes processing grief more intense and challenging. People are more able to engage with their loss when they have a structured way to do so. But do these behaviors actually help people feel better?

Behavioral scientists Michael Norton and Francesca Gino conducted a series of experiments to explore this question. In the first study, the researchers split participants into two groups. Members of one group were instructed to reflect on the death of a loved one or the end of a close relationship. Members of the other group were instructed to reflect on the same loss, but they were also asked to write about a ritual they engaged in after the loss.

Those who wrote about their post-loss rituals reported lower levels of grief and reduced feelings of a lack of control. The researchers' conclusion? Rituals restore a sense of control after people lose loved ones. And when they feel more in control, their grief eases. Moreover, those who described a personal ritual also felt less aggrieved, meaning that just thinking about the ritual helped people feel better.

But does the type of loss matter? Can rituals ease disappointment from the loss of something more mundane? In their next experiment, Norton and Gino invited college students to participate in a lottery where one person won two hundred dollars, leaving the rest with a sudden sense of loss.

To make the loss more relevant, before the winner was chosen, participants were asked to write an essay about why they wanted to win and how they would spend the money. After the winning number was drawn, the winner left the room, and the remaining participants were divided into two groups, one that would engage in a ritual and one that would proceed without ritual. The members of the ritual group were asked to do the following:

Step 1. Please draw how you currently feel on the piece of paper on your desk for two minutes.

Step 2. Please sprinkle a pinch of salt on the paper with your drawing.

Step 3. Please tear up the piece of paper.

Step 4. Now please count up to ten in your head five times.

At the same time, the non-ritual group only drew their feelings. Everyone then completed a questionnaire measuring their perceived control and grief. The results showed that those who performed a ritual after something as ordinary as losing a lottery felt less upset about the loss. While random rituals may seem impractical, the intention of eased grief or belonging to a community may suffice for the ritual to work.

During those moments where life seems hard, those times when all you can do is eat, sleep, and breathe, you can lean on rituals to help quiet anxiety and develop a practice of intentionality: how you want to live, what you want to remember, and how you want to feel.

These symbolic behaviors honor what you have lost in separation, help you let go of what you can't control, and provide the strength for you to open yourself to support from others. When you're in the middle of emotional turmoil, it's comforting to have a plan of action to face the disruption head-on and know what's coming up next.

How we manage through loss relies on our narratives—the stories we tell about the person or experience we have lost, our explanations around what happened, and the memories and hidden beliefs that we often accept unchallenged. We can unpack our narratives and clarify how we want to engage with the world, then create rituals that meet our needs.

Engaging in rituals during loss and separation is more than a portal to ease sadness and grief—it's also motivating and expansive. The power of rituals is in their simplicity. Done with intention, rituals are not just about closing a part of your life; they're about integrating your past into your dreams and aspirations.

◆   ◆   ◆

"I'm not great. I can't get him out of my mind." With polite smiles and restless energy, Sofia sits across from me. Though raw and reassembling, she has a quiet intensity in the way she carries her instability. One year after a breakup with someone she thought was her forever person, Sofia has come to my office feeling underequipped to manage the loss.

Brandon, her ex-boyfriend, still lingers in her thoughts. They met in graduate school, then reconnected years later and maintained a long-distance relationship built on daily calls and emotional honesty—something rare for her. Seemingly out of the blue, he ended it; he blocked her number and didn't answer emails.

"I knew everything about him. One day, we were talking about him moving to Chicago to live with me, and the next day he told me he no longer wanted to be with me." Softness visibly transforms into a distanced bitterness. "I'll never know why he ended it like that after two years."

Sofia has become despondent. She moves more slowly and has difficulty finding words; she has little motivation and energy to guide her during the day. Micro-conversations with colleagues and neighbors dwindle, as she can't be bothered to engage, preferring to stay home pretending to work as she surfs the internet, often visiting his social media pages, memorizing his posts, and gazing at photos into which she mentally inserts herself.

As Sofia rewatches past video footage in her mind, she unknowingly edits out major arguments and smooths over gridlock. But after she bathes in the good old times, lost in the sense of comfort and love surrounding her back then, the reality hits her: The relationship is gone forever—or, worse, it was never there to begin with. She realizes she can't ever go back in time. Separation and loss render her resistant to change. It's hard for her to move forward when she's stuck in times gone by.

Bittersweet Pull to Return

Our minds instinctively reach backward when we're faced with uncertainty, loneliness, or overwhelm or when we're unsure of who we are, sometimes on a daily basis. Whether we recognize it or not, we will all be pulled to our pasts at some point. When people become parents for the first time, the relentless demands of a newborn lead many to long for their pre-baby lives. When a long-term relationship ends in another dissatisfying gridlock of arguments, people reminisce about past relationships where they felt more competent, loved, and respected, sweeping aside the various reasons why said relationship ended in the first place. With nostalgia, people dream about the predictable rhythm of old workplaces, selectively erasing memories of competitive colleagues who belittled them.

Despite how common this pull to return is, most people have no way to manage it other than by venting to friends and family about the predicament, exhausting themselves and anyone who's willing to listen.

This pull to return isn't always a bad thing. It can give you a way of thinking about who you are and help make sense of what's happening in the present day. There's a possibility of life getting better because it's been good before. The common denominator underlying the pull to return is a desire for life to feel better. You want something to be hopeful for. But nostalgia is bittersweet—sweet with a sense of love and warmth, and bitter because it no longer exists.

Across the world and time, people have had a longing for the past. Loss becomes unbearable; a longing for the past is part of the universal human experience. Studies show that we're more often pulled to the past when we're faced with psychological threats: feeling lonely, sad, with low self-worth or existential blues.

We don't want to separate. Major stressors threaten to shatter who we know ourselves to be—our identities, our virtues, our senses of self and belonging. So a pull to a more favorable time in our lives comes in handy when we're overwhelmed.

Yet when we're experiencing the pull to the past, we're longing for a time that never actually existed. The brain selectively chooses and modifies the past to make it seem far better than it was by using a selective *positivity bias.* The past becomes a highlights reel that plays on a loop while the bloopers mysteriously disappear because your mind blocks out the negative and emphasizes the positive.

In the face of social isolation, loneliness, or disconnection, you are pulled to remember the good times, and that shapes how you process your current situation. A familiar scent, item, person, or situation can pull you into the past because you need some kind of emotional comfort and crave stability, not separation. The present time is too unbearable, and you aren't sure how to improve the situation. You may feel trapped or lured to a familiar feeling—even if it's not healthy.

Whether it's pining for a romance from your high-school years, remembering the scent of a loved one who passed away, or absorbing a sense of connection when thinking about your hometown, your brain is engaging in a complex interplay of systems. In an orchestra of neurotransmitters and brain structures, a pull to the past helps you navigate psychological threats.

But here's where it gets interesting: The pull to return to the past isn't just focused on getting you through the day. Like an emotional stabilizer, a pull to the past acts like a psychological immune response that kicks in when you feel lonely, meaningless, or unsteady about your identity. It's a psychological resource the brain calls upon to counter present challenges. Returning to a past time helps preserve your self-esteem and build a coherent narrative about your life.

So your nostalgia probably isn't just escaping from threats to sunnier times. Your brain is likely actively making meaning from the past, attempting to integrate difficult emotions rather than stamp them out. You aren't just remembering the past; you're building a neurochemical bridge between who you were and who you are.

Binding Across Time and Space

The pull to the past opens an opportunity for insightful self-reflection, curiosity, and productive exploration. In that pull to return is a gold mine of information, connecting you to your values, identities, relationships, and places of belonging. Unfortunately, most of the time people do the opposite and sink into their regrets.

"Maybe I should have fought more to stay with him," Sofia laments. "He was my best friend, and I don't know if I can connect with someone like that again." When she compares her past with her present, the pain of loss becomes too much to bear. Tangled in rejection, her heartbreak entwines yearning with a sense of possession: She was his and he was hers. Until they weren't.

Having avoided engagement in most of her life, she contracts the lens of her world until her only view is of her relationship with Brandon. With little else occupying her life, she has nothing to do but consume herself with memories of him.

The thought of him is enough of an intermittent reward to keep her brain hooked. Future-oriented fantasies with her first love and past-oriented regrets begin to interfere in her life. She can't engage in real-world relationships since she's sustaining a separate one in her mind.

Sofia's eyes meet mine, but as she speaks, there is something deeply missing: responsibility. While she acknowledges the breakup, her view of the demise of the relationship centers on him being selfish, immature, and more focused on his career than the relationship with her. On a logical level, she believes they would not make a good pairing.

Yet she continues to romanticize their past into the present, holding on to it to numb the sting of loneliness and soften the spotlight on reality. I want to explore the reasons for the break, to understand if there were major relational injuries that we could focus on, but I can sense she isn't quite ready for deep self-reflection. So I engage with her where she's at—her present suffering.

It becomes clear that Sofia's heartbreak isn't just about the loss of Brandon. It's about the disruption in her identity. When a meaningful relationship ends, you don't only miss the person but the shared imagined future and the version of yourself you were. The rituals, inside jokes, and emotional anchoring. This is the lingering pain of heartbreak, as it shakes the foundation of how you see yourself, not just how you feel. Sofia wasn't just grieving love but the life she was building around that love.

SUZAN SONG, MD, PHD

Sofia is continuously pulled to her past in an attachment withdrawal of dopamine and oxytocin as she obsessively replays the relationship: *What if I had said this differently? What if he hadn't done that?* But research shows that this kind of counterfactual thinking can delay healing by keeping you stuck in a hypothetical version of reality. She's left wondering, *Who am I now without him?*, which makes sense, as relationships shape who we are. She's having a legitimate identity crisis.

I engage Sofia in a simple ritual to honor the past and allow her to integrate into the present. The goal isn't for her to "get over" the breakup. The aim is for her to grow through it. First, I have her tell me about the past relationship (the release) to acknowledge what she appreciated, name what hurt, and say what she wished she and Brandon understood about each other. Then to say goodbye.

Second, I have her tell me what she would tell her future self (the rebuild), to confirm what she learned about herself from the relationship, define what values or needs she now sees more clearly, and commit to a boundary or truth she wants to honor going forward. We end with her integrating the past as she moves into the present and future self.

Third, I encourage her to use a tangible cue for a psychological shift in representing the transition—she chooses to buy a small plant for herself to symbolize her growth from the experience. I also ask her to engage in one small action that marks the beginning of the next version of herself. It doesn't have to be bold; it just has to be hers. She chooses to sign up for a pottery class she's always wanted to take, organizes a weekend getaway with a college friend, and creates a new playlist of uplifting music.

Her ritual offers a structured way to hold grief while making way for growth—an approach grounded in science. Reflecting on the past relationship (privately or through a letter) promotes cognitive closure and narrative coherence, helping to externalize ruminative thoughts and open space for new emotional patterns.

By honoring the positive and painful aspects of the experience, the brain can more fully engage in emotional integration, reducing lingering stress. And engaging in a concrete task reinforces behav-

ioral commitment—signaling to the self that change isn't only possible but already underway.

It turns out that for Sofia, this simple ritual to honor and let go
was highly effective in shifting her attention and commitments
from the past toward the present. While she still thinks of Brandon,
she refocuses on accepting and honoring who she was in the relationship to create space for a new one. Loss doesn't erase growth.
Having conversations with your future or past self can give you perspective and help you reconnect with who you know yourself to be.

Rituals like this can be used to honor those we have lost and give
structure to our grieving by binding us to others and to ourselves
across time and space. They help connect us to the people we care
about and to the love we feel—it doesn't just turn off because the
person is no longer present. Losses can be memorialized through
rituals, providing a sense of control and structure to our sadness
while keeping our sense of self intact.

Drifting

Rituals can clearly help us process loss, whether it's grieving a loved
one or feeling briefly disappointed about losing the lottery. But loss
doesn't always present in obvious forms. Sometimes it shows as
uncertainty—a quiet nagging sense that we've drifted off course and
we don't know what to do next in our romantic relationships, in our
careers, or within our families. Unlike traditional mourning, this
kind of loss doesn't come with a clear road map. There's no funeral
for an abandoned career path or sympathy cards for questioning
one's purpose.

Losing your sense of direction—wondering if you're on the
wrong path or when you're struggling to make a major decision—
can create the same emotional turbulence as more tangible losses. In
a way, it's the loss of a stable identity, the messy unraveling of who
you thought you were or who you imagined you would be.

Studies show that when people lack clarity about the future, the
brain reacts as if it's experiencing a breakup. That sense of drifting,

of not knowing where to go next, activates the same neural circuits involved in processing grief. When adrift, many people arrive at my office in knots of angst as they try to develop specific goals—what exact job or position they want, whether they should stay or go in a relationship and what the timeline should be, et cetera. Demanding answers, they constantly ask themselves, *What do I want?*, then sink into despair when a specific solution doesn't rise to the top.

For many, these questions are problematic. Motivated and driven, many people journal away to try and find out why they're unhappy in their dream job or why they are frustrated with relationships, only to circle back steeped in dissatisfaction. What they miss is a crucial question: *How do I want to feel?*

Sure, some people need support in turning specific goals into action. But most people are trying to solve problems before knowing the question. Starting with how you want to feel and working backward allows you to tap into the more flexible thinking needed to open paths you might not have seen before.

If you are uncomfortable journaling about your deepest feelings, try to ritualize what I call an "emotional GPS," similar to a gratitude journal. While studies are clear on the benefits of gratitude, I've found that at times, a singular focus on gratitude can minimize real struggles and encourage a form of toxic positivity, avoiding or suppressing the agonizing but needed emotions.

Instead, try making three columns on a piece of paper. Identify three feelings you want to experience more often. I'll use the examples of *proud, inspired,* and *loved.* In column one, think of what you were proud of today, something that you did that made you proud. In column two, write down something that inspired you today. And in column three, consider a time during the day when you felt loved. Here's my journal from last night as an example:

Proud.	Inspired.	Loved.
Teaching my kids to knit	Hearing a friend give a presentation	When a neighbor checked in on me during a snowstorm

Your emotional GPS doesn't require lots of words, but it guides your feelings to spark a release of serotonin (the well-being hormone released when you feel proud), dopamine (the reward hormone released when you feel inspired), and oxytocin (the cuddle hormone released when you feel loved).

This kind of journal is just one example of how we can use narratives and stories to navigate life using emotions as internal guidance signals—not distractions. Just as a GPS recalibrates your route when you're off track, your desired emotional signals can redirect you toward what's meaningful, fulfilling, and aligned with who you really are.

Rituals are more than routines; they are anchors in the storm of uncertainty. Whether you are mourning the loss of a loved one, shaking off the sting of a minor setback, or searching for clarity in the midst of a career crossroads, rituals help bridge the gap between what was and what comes next.

They don't erase loss or hand over immediate answers, but they offer something just as powerful: the sense that you are not adrift, that you have a way forward, even if you can't yet see the destination. In a world that often feels unpredictable, rituals remind you that you still have agency—not over everything, but over how you respond, how you rebuild, and how you find meaning in the spaces between endings and beginnings.

Action Tools for Separation and Loss

A. Make Meaning Out of Loss

1. Use rituals to provide scaffolding. Rituals give structure to the chaos of life and restore a sense of control and meaning during times of separation and loss. Whether you're grieving a loved one or disappointed by a missed opportunity, rituals can turn emotional disorientation into coherence.

2. Design an ending that honors your growth. Rituals help us process separation and loss through honoring and integrating what was and scaffolding transition into a new identity. Loss can fragment identity, but ritual can reassemble it. Consider ritualizing remembering, since grief isn't linear. The grief may not change, but your relationship to it can. Release and rebuild to create space to reflect on lessons learned from a lost relationship, job, or time in your life.

B. Anchor Yourself with Others

3. Engage in collective recovery. Separation and loss are destabilizing universal experiences. People around the world turn to rituals for relief, so consider grieving with others. Rituals that are rooted in community validate pain and restore connection. What cultural or collective rituals are you currently engaged in? Are there any you would like to develop with your community?

4. Create a reliable touchstone with others. If you're feeling a loss of psychological safety due to societal upheaval, choose an anchor hour every week to unplug from media and external noise and create a reliable touchstone with others—walks, cooking together, engaging in community-service projects, listening to music, or engaging in a faith tradition. These rituals can act as a symbol of agency in an unpredictable world.

C. Bridge Who You Were with Who You're Becoming

5. Return to what grounds you. In times of separation and loss, reengage with the people, places, and practices that made you who you are. Speak to your former self, then give voice to your current thoughts and feelings to integrate your identities. Speak to the person you want to become and revisit them when you need clarity.

6. Integrate your story. When life feels disjointed, rituals can help you weave a coherent narrative about who you are across time. Honor your past self by not burying or chastising former versions of yourself; recognize and embrace them as chapters that got you here.

7. Lean on your emotional GPS. Each day, reflect on what made you feel proud, loved, and inspired—three core emotional cues tied to motivation, connection, and meaning. Allow these feelings to guide your mind toward what matters. Just like a GPS recalibrates your route when you're off track, your emotional signals can redirect you toward what gives you energy, connection, and purpose.

5

Liminal Spaces:
Letting Go

A few years ago, I developed a fascination with anklets made with bright threads and tied in a knot that I soaked in nail polish or glue in an attempt to make them permanent. Until then, I hadn't worn much jewelry; maybe a wedding band and stud earrings at most.

But that was before I was divorced and co-parenting two children. If you had met me when I was forty-three, you would have thought I had it all—you might even have felt a twinge of jealousy. My four- and five-year-olds and I went to the local farm twice a week to pet our friend Oreo the goat, bump along on a tractor ride, and pick ripe peaches.

I was married, had a minivan and an incredibly flexible job in academia where I was supported by the chair of my department, who put me forward for full professorship. Although I paused my traveling to be with the kids, I still consulted for various humanitarian agencies around the world. I owned a house, hosted moms' groups and book clubs, and baked cookie bars for school fundraisers.

Throughout my twenties, I had had a series of years-long relationships with good people. But I always felt that I'd been swept into them, never quite choosing the relationships but rather floating along with whoever was interested in me.

That was, until California. Having just ended a long-term relationship with my best friend turned boyfriend, I was now a thirty-year-old single woman in a new city, unattached, and looking forward to my clinical fellowship.

Lured by near-perfect daily weather that let me bike more often than drive, I landed in Palo Alto, California, and was distracted by frozen yogurt shops and majestic redwood trees just an hour away. Gone were the interminable winters with bitter cold that cut to the bone and the eighty- to one-hundred-hour workweeks in Boston. When I first saw the natural beauty of Northern California, it was so breathtaking, I thought I might pass out. I was standing tall, chasing excitement and adventure in everything and everyone.

During my first weekend, I arrived late to a wedding reception and met one of the only single people there. I was eager to explore the area, and we talked about hikes around the Bay Area and favorite coffee-shop hangouts. I didn't think much of him, as he seemed more of a tour guide than anything else. Until he mentioned something that drew me in for the next four years: He avoided going to the doctor.

Now, many of you might get swept off your feet in the bloom of genuine adoration or by an intangible connection of pheromones. I got there eventually, but that wasn't the initial hook. For me, I saw someone who needed to be saved—just like my father. But this time, the person was someone I could care for and protect which would make up for the fact that I couldn't do so for my father.

Of course I wasn't aware of this at the time. My growth asked for more than the relationship could take, so we parted ways after about four years. I had been blind to the reality of who he was, clinging instead to the ideas I projected on him. Now I was a thirty-four-year-old single woman. I had completed my clinical training and was more aware than ever of the shelf life of my ovaries: I wanted kids, and I wanted them yesterday.

There wasn't much time to grieve the relationship—my biological clock was ticking. So I got down to business and spent much of my savings to freeze my eggs so I could date without pressure. Aware of my repetition compulsion, I wanted to have time to break the pattern and I didn't want to jump into a relationship just to have a child.

I spent a couple of years of exploring, dating, traveling, and kite-surfing, embracing the single life. I dated someone long-distance for about five months, and then the unimaginable happened: I became pregnant.

Here I was, a thirty-seven-year-old woman who really wanted children (*I study children and families, for goodness' sake!*), now pregnant. But my joy at finally expecting a child was tangled with a decision I hadn't considered: Should I marry someone just because I got pregnant?

To be fair, I told myself it was a bad idea more than a few times, but I didn't heed my own advice. One has to be humble in the face of second-trimester hormones. And nobody else was warning me off this course of action. Immersed in the narrative ideal of a romantic tale and a storybook family, I got married.

Two kids, one bunny, and seven years later, I got divorced. Now with the biggest loves of my life (who had turned five and six years old) and living back on the East Coast to be closer to family, I found myself wondering, *What did I do to cause such upheaval?* My life had the plot twists and romance arcs of a Korean drama, but I was still stuck in the sad part where a car accident blinds someone.

The decision to marry was tangled—influenced by fear, timing, and the weight of what felt like the right thing to do. But when I found out I was pregnant, there was rare clarity. However complicated the beginning, my love for the children never has been. Watching them become who they are has been one of the greatest privileges of my life. They have pulled me into a kind of love that reorients your entire world—where everything else quiets so you don't miss a moment of who they are becoming.

So the first weekend that my children were with their father, I sat buzzing with a primal terror in my bones; the silence in the house was deafening. The separation from my kids, who had never been away from me for one night, sparked a flurry of unexpected grief:

the sudden loss of my father, the separation from past loves, and, now, the loss of a narrative of a nuclear family and someone to grow old with.

Clinicians call this *cumulative* or *compounded grief,* where a new loss, even if seemingly small, can trigger a grief from past losses to intensify the pain. It felt primally wrong not to be able to tuck my kids into bed at night, as if the universe weren't spinning properly on its axis or I was floating in space, untethered and alone. Because I was.

Anyone who cares for children is aware that parenting is a practice of letting go. Initially, it's letting go of your own independence and identity as yourself-without-kids and letting go of the need to overextend yourself. For a mother, it's trying to breastfeed your babies as long as possible and making sure no one wakes them from a nap or disrupts their schedules.

Later, it's letting go of unattainable expectations around homemade fondant birthday cakes and about getting your pre-baby body back, as well as letting go of controlling what they eat, who they play with, and how they dress. As they enter adolescence, you have to let go of a supervisory parenting style and become more of a coach, mindful of your own emotional reactivity and letting go of a need for your teens to behave a certain way.

There's another layer of letting go: when your children move out of the house, for college, a job, boarding school, or to serve in the military. Cue the guttural cries. Parents across college campuses linger a little too long on move-in day, knowing that when they leave, they'll be leaving pieces of their hearts behind. But parents assure themselves when they return home and view their teen's now empty room, *This is how it's supposed to be.*

But the separation from children through divorce speeds up the parenting process of letting go. Guilt over doing something that potentially messed up my children mingled with worry about how they'd come out on the other side in adulthood. I sat paralyzed, waiting to see them again.

I was exhausted but couldn't sleep. I had so much work to do, but

I couldn't focus. Listless and internally twisted in knots, I yearned for something to ease the liminal space. For me, a small reprieve came in the form of an anklet.

Colorful friendship bracelets with little heart charms or faux leather bands entwined with turtles—I wore them on my left ankle, often hidden enough to be missed but also peeking out enough to be noticed as quirky.

A man next to me in yoga class glanced at my ankle during a down-dog. *My anklet must make me look twenty years younger,* I thought. A woman in my book club did a double take as she reached across the couch for her glass of merlot. *Maybe she's thinking that I'm stuck in the wrong fashion decade.* People glanced or stared, but no one asked why I wore them, what was going on.

My anklet helped me feel connected to the kids—it was a transitional object, like a child's blankie or tattered stuffy. Every time we traveled, the kids and I had a ritual where we chose an anklet to wear in the future.

When I missed them, I spun the anklet for an oxytocin surge, the equivalent of pulling up photos of my kids on my phone to feel instant love and compassion. Guilt over blowing up their Daniel Tiger family abated. It reminded me that what mattered to them was to have a mom who was responsible and accountable, loving and patient—not only to them, but to herself.

Ambiguous Loss

Separation from my children created suffering in part due to something psychologists call *ambiguous loss*—the limbo of someone who is in your mind but physically absent or physically present but emotionally gone. Chances are, you've had an ambiguous loss. If you've ever experienced a breakup or divorce, had a miscarriage, emigrated, had a parent with an addiction, lost someone to suicide, or were estranged from a loved one, you've felt the instability of losing a physical or emotional connection.

As a psychology graduate student in the 1970s, Pauline Boss was interested in the psychological effects of fathers who were physically present but emotionally or psychologically elsewhere. This was the time of the Vietnam War, and when she gave a presentation of her dissertation to military personnel, they asked, "What about those families of missing-in-action soldiers in Vietnam, men who are psychologically present but physically absent?" This question captured her curiosity, and she eventually focused her studies on what she later called *ambiguous loss*.

Threatening our sense of stability, ambiguous loss defies our instincts to resolve or fix. Our sense of comfort in the world depends on our ability to predict our future. We feel as though we're going crazy with uncertainty. Sometimes stressors are so overwhelming that they short-circuit the mind's ability to process and register what's going on. Unanswered questions leave an underlying buzz—something isn't right. You go blank and can't find your way out of this one, as there's no clear path forward and no way to control the outcome.

Ambiguous loss is rooted in relationships—attachments to loved ones past and present are threatened. The strain also endangers your connection to yourself—your self-esteem, identity, and sense of psychological safety. Breakups and divorces, international moves, military deployment, brain injury, addiction, and incarceration of loved ones all challenge your connections to support, and destabilize your sense of self. Rituals can help you engage with the ambiguity and let go of the need for certainty.

◆ ◆ ◆

One pleasant spring day, Omar arrived at his parents' home to celebrate their twenty-fifth wedding anniversary. When he walked through the front door, he immediately stiffened at what he saw: socks. They were everywhere in the house—hanging from the key holder, sitting on top of the toilet, inside the shower. They weren't celebratory decorations or works of abstract art. They reflected a new worrisome pattern of his father's behavior due to Alzheimer's dementia.

Omar had often had a tense relationship with his father over the years, arguing over how money was spent or the qualities to look for in a life partner. They didn't show each other affection, tell each other secrets, or discuss their concerns. Though both were quick to gossip and dispense unsolicited advice, they rarely spoke about the important things, never said "I'm struggling" or "I love you." At the same time, there was a tacit understanding that they had each other's backs. Their relationship often stretched but never broke.

Until now. I've been seeing Omar in psychotherapy for four years, from his single days to being swept away in love, from job changes to new parenthood. I've been impressed with the security with which he moves through transitions. Yet the loss of his father looms large.

Omar faces a difficult predicament: His father is still alive and lives thirty minutes from Omar and his wife and their one-year-old son. Over the past year, his father's old self has suffered a slow death because of the Alzheimer's. He's still able to remember the names of loved ones but can't always recognize common things in his house. His day-to-day life is relatively full of intermittent confusion and disorientation, and he often makes things up. "It's like my whole childhood and relationship with him are being erased in large chunks," Omar murmurs. Like a doppelgänger, his father has the same body but none of the same mannerisms or ways of thinking or behaving. It's jarring.

"I can't believe I'm about to say this, but I think it would be a lot easier if he died. It's too much to have him changing into a completely different person right before me. I can't know how bad it's going to get and when to just let him die in my mind," he confesses.

Omar is stuck in liminality, having left one place but not yet arrived at the next. Confusingly, he feels the loss of the father he remembers while his father is still alive and next to him.

Ambiguity is destructive in part because it challenges our drive for certainty. Most people don't want to tolerate problems with no solutions. As humans, we look for what we can do to solve the issue.

We want to fix problems, get over hardships quickly, and choose a path of happiness over pain.

The goal becomes getting definitive answers—someone is dead or alive; here or gone. This hunger for solutions is admirable, as it launched humanity into the Industrial Age and advanced technology and the medical field.

The problem is, sometimes there's no attainable solution—especially when it comes to relationships. Many people are constantly told "You can change the world!" and "Your destiny is in your hands if you work hard enough!" So it's no surprise that when a loved one is estranged or gone without contact, people try to find ways to take back control.

Wanting as much control as possible makes sense, as it's hard to live with unresolved grief for years and even decades. Studies show that chronically living with unwavering uncertainty is associated with anxiety, depression, guilt, helplessness, and even substance abuse and interpersonal violence.

Yet ambiguous loss tends to be complex in nature, with no clear-cut solutions. It's often not even seen by society as something to grieve, so people question the validity of their suffering. *Why is this affecting me so much? Is there something wrong with me for not being able to manage this? Why can't others see my suffering?* They try to move through their daily lives as coherently as possible, though it's now with a simmering internal agitation.

Challenge the Drive for Certainty

Whether it's the end of a romantic relationship, sending children off to college, losing a baby to miscarriage, moving across the world, or supporting a loved one with dementia, ambiguous loss weighs on the soul more heavily than most of us would like to admit. This kind of loss affects people in three main ways: by overwhelming emotions, challenging relationships, and immobilizing them.

Feeling incompetent and out of control, Omar blames himself for not being able to fix the problem and is weighed down by self-reproach, feeling stuck and blocked by the universe. His wife and friends aren't quite sure how to support him through this. If his father had died, they would have a cultural script—they'd attend the funeral, send flowers, and bring dinners.

But now? He's grieving, but there's no concrete death. People aren't sure how to show up for him, so they don't. Feeling alone, Omar is confused about how to manage the deep pain and bitterness of mourning a person who is still alive. For Omar, the hard part isn't dealing with his father's physical loss. It's figuring out how to live with him.

Suffering from a chronic sense of unknowing that defies logic, how can Omar resist the urge to wall himself off from the world? I have found ambiguity to be one of the major causes of instability; it makes even the most accomplished, confident, and kindest people hide from life.

When Grief Freezes

Ambiguity preoccupies us and leaves us stuck in uncertainty. It challenges our logical reasoning. In an effort to avoid a potential loss—of status, security, a sense of feeling loved, or certainty of an identity—people run around in circles, out of breath with tattered shoes, unable to take a different course of action.

Overwhelmed with anxiety and confusion about how they should respond to the situation, they become paralyzed. Unsure how to talk with friends and family, they stumble in their words and thoughts. They aren't sure what to say, how to say it, or even if they should say anything at all. Not only are they unable to communicate with others—they don't know what they're supposed to tell themselves.

This is a neurobiological response. In the face of stress, the autonomic nervous system activates toward *fight* (ever been irritable or short-tempered with a loved one or colleague?), *flight* (*Let's just go to the movies and pretend this never happened*), or *freeze* (numbing out and streaming shows you don't remember the plots of an hour later).

In all these cases, your nervous system activates under stress, and the fear center of the brain activates for survival, at times shutting down the thinking part of your brain—the cortex. If you've ever had someone tell you to calm down and breathe when you're a twelve out of ten on an anger scale, you're aware that when your limbic system is on fire, you can't think. Nothing computes.

If someone has physically died, there's a little more language for your inner dialogue. If you're religious, you might try to comfort yourself with *They're now in a better place*. If you had a good relationship with the person, you can tell yourself, *At least we shared our love for each other.*

It's hard to make those internal statements when you just don't know where your loved one is or how they are doing. The normal ways of coping no longer work, as you're psychologically immobilized—you don't know what you're supposed to do with your time or how to engage in life. Omar decides to avoid his father as much as possible. Grief freezes.

To Engage or Avoid?

When we're struggling with instabilities in our lives, it's often not only the actual event that's difficult—it's also how we think about it. Our narratives become the shields or the swords to our suffering. For many people, the first response is to cut and run—avoid the situation and the associated feelings as much as possible and keep moving: *Ignore. Keep yourself occupied so you don't have to think about it.*

Other times, sufferers believe they need to constantly engage and confront the conflict. *What if there's something I can do to make things better? How can I possibly move on with daily life?* If Omar engages too much with the realities of the situation, at some point he'll become so stressed as to be nonfunctioning. So in the face of high-intensity, long-lasting uncertainty, is it better to engage or avoid?

In theory, engaging with a dilemma is healthy. Research suggests that various ways to engage—problem-solving, accepting a situation, or changing one's perspective on it—are generally viewed as beneficial. In practice, though, that's not always true. You've seen people engage with a conflict only to spiral into a tense gridlock with even more heightened anger, or devolving to hopelessness.

When we don't know what the short- or long-term future is going to be, we try to find as much information as we can to shrink the unknown. People around the world get trapped into this dance of how much, when, and whether to engage with life struggles and they often feel ineffective or not good enough when they can't improve the situation.

While research shows that coping with the stressor through wishful thinking and denial aren't helpful, studies also show that there are indeed situations in which distractions can be useful: when the situation is too difficult to engage in, when it is high-intensity, or when there's long-lasting uncertainty.

Distraction can prevent you from getting trapped in helplessness and unproductive rumination in situations over which you have little control. It can help you stay focused, clearer-minded, and open to finding calm or even moments of joy in your daily life. I think of it as the pressure valve that allows one to continue to engage without exploding or getting burned.

But a major problem with distraction is that it is often a proxy for avoidance. You may think that not thinking about the issue and pretending it's not a part of your life is a form of healthy distraction— until you realize you never actually revisited the issue in a productive way.

Distraction and avoidance aren't the same. Taking a walk in nature, listening to music you love, or having tea with a friend are distractions that induce positive feelings. These *positive distractions* help you think about or engage in a beneficial activity to ease difficult emotions and stop ruminations. They're actually a gateway coping strategy, as they lead to problem-focused coping rather than avoiding. So rest assured, your painting, rock climbing, or strumming on the guitar is likely good for you.

Despite the research showing that knowing how to positively distract yourself is an essential life skill, most of us overlook it. The problem starts early: Children are told to focus, pay attention, not to daydream or be distracted from schoolwork. We direct children's attention away from their play and limit their time with friends despite the research that shows that positive distractions can improve behavioral and emotional well-being and reduce stress and anxiety.

Playing a board game, dancing like no one's watching, and even folding your laundry and rearranging a room in your house does more than just lower your anxiety; it also helps you address problems more effectively. Ruminating about the same conflict repeatedly with no progress only increases suffering. Positive distraction breaks the cycle of habitually dwelling on the same issue and gives you a conscious time-out so you can engage with the issue when you have more energy.

Meaning Without Mastery

It's hard to engage in avoidance when you're talking with a therapist. We have a way of inviting patients into conversations they would otherwise not have. After Omar rattles off the list of people he's frustrated with—various medical providers, his father, and other family members—he gives voice to the narratives that are likely more constant in his mind but that he hasn't wanted to air: "I feel like a bad son. I don't want to spend time with him—I don't know how to." He continues rapidly, "I'm the only child. I need to be able to manage this but I can't. I've got my own life I need to focus on."

Omar is trapped in a vicious cycle. He attempts to use logic to figure out how he is at fault and how he has failed to live up to his own expectations of himself. Every time he looks at his parents, he feels either guilty or ill-equipped to manage the situation.

Your narratives—your perspectives, meanings, and explanations for what's happening in your life—are your reality. Meaning involves explanations of experiences; mastery is having a sense of control over forces that affect one's life. Grieving the loss of a beloved who is alive but different challenges your ability to make meaning.

People try to find ways to instill meaning and logic into narratives. When they don't have control over information that they're desperate for, they move toward the anger that comes from confusion or ruminate on how ineffective they are in accepting the situation—both viewpoints make them feel more powerful, even if the anger is self-directed.

Defining Ambiguity

Omar is caught in an emotional crossfire; every visit to his father leaves him with a mixture of sorrow and shame. While he hates seeing his dad like this, the idea of not showing up feels like betrayal. In the space between who his father was and who he has become, Omar is losing pieces of himself too.

What helps isn't clarity but reframing the problem as one of ambiguity. It's normal for ambiguity to lead to conflicted emotions. Defining the problem as ambiguity allows you to shift away from self-blame and a desire to control that which you cannot, and toward identifying the problem that you can actually have some mastery over: how to balance ambiguity and helplessness.

We often talk about closure as if it's a door we've shut. But with ambiguous loss, the door never quite closes. What you *can* do is build a new room around it with meaning and memory. Omar is a former musician, so I ask him to create a playlist of songs that represent different emotional touchpoints: songs that his father loved, songs that remind Omar of his father, songs that he wishes his father could hear now, and songs that reflect his grief as well as his growth.

To my surprise, Omar takes to this and listens to his playlist before and after every encounter with his father. Pairing music with intentional reflection helps him access and release unspoken grief. Tapping into nonverbal emotional processing, this ritual eases his ruminations about a resolution and gives him the structure and self-direction to stay connected to himself and his father.

When Omar begins to ask not what he owes but what his father might want from him, something shifts. His father's love hasn't disappeared, only transformed. Omar gives himself permission to reclaim his own life. The ritual integrates the pain so he doesn't have to ignore it, and it gives him a path of connection while also letting him move forward.

Omar still feels overwhelmed with heartache and longs for a future with his father that will never be, but he allows himself to embrace his present-day father more and opens himself to experiencing joys in life without guilt.

Universal yet rarely acknowledged, ambiguity is one of the most difficult forms of instability to experience. Whether it's due to the loss of someone still living or the physical absence of someone still close to your heart, ambiguity can tear down your ability to cope. The loss can be so destabilizing that it feels impossible to control any part of the ambiguity. But in the face of complicated loss, rituals can serve as a way to let go of what was and create space for what is. Using rituals to foster a sense of mastery can help offset the feeling of powerlessness.

Unresolved Goodbyes

Kateryna had always been thankful for her life—even during the struggles of parenthood. Though content with her career as a librarian in a city in Ukraine, she found her greatest satisfaction in her family.

Due to a hereditary condition, she was told it was unlikely she would be able to become pregnant, but miraculously, she did, and she and her husband, Dimitri, welcomed their daughter, Natalia, into the world. Strong-willed and always pushing boundaries, Natalia thrived on little sleep. In kindergarten, she jumped off a swing in an attempt to fly and fractured her wrist. In second grade, she painted a mural on the side of the family's newly washed car.

In 2014, when Natalia was nine years old, the Russo-Ukrainian war began. Her parents placed her in boarding school in a safer area nearby. Despite the ongoing tension around her, the family still lived in peace.

That is, until February 2022, when Russia's full-scale offensive killed or injured thousands of civilians. Violating a litany of international humanitarian laws, occupying forces launched indiscriminate and disproportionate bombing and shelling of civilian areas, including homes, schools, and health-care facilities. Armed groups occupied parts of Ukraine, looting property and subjecting civilians to torture, executions, sexual violence, and enforced disappearances.

Natalia was at a summer camp when occupying forces laid siege to the area; children ran from the bombings, following neighbors and other groups heading west to a safer part of Ukraine. Instead of finding safety, Natalia was stopped at a checkpoint and put on a bus, and family members have not heard from her since.

Natalia became one of the 19,500 deported children over the course of that year. According to reports, children forcibly removed from Ukraine are forbidden to speak Ukrainian, practice religions they were raised in, and communicate with family; they are given new passports and entered into an adoption system that erases their past identities.

Determined to find her daughter, Kateryna spent most hours of the day talking to various community-based and international organizations as well as reporters from around the world who might have information on how to find her daughter.

After six months, Kateryna struggled to find stable footing. Her demands to know where her daughter was became louder and more vehement. Worn out, deprived of the answers she was looking for and unable to control the situation, Kateryna sought support from a therapist, a colleague of mine who reached out for consultation.

"The injustice is infuriating," Kateryna states in anguish. "I should have watched her better. I should have been stricter with her." Agonizing and full of self-reproach, Kateryna freezes in paralysis. Thinking isn't an option—rages of fear and sadness shut down her ability to process anything. She tries to reframe and redirect her thoughts, but within five minutes she becomes saturated in a maternal grief that seeps deep into her core. Powerlessness takes over, and her only option is to avoid. Helplessness is contagious, as her therapist also feels stuck and unsure of how to help.

What enables people who are going through major setbacks to find balance? Time and distance may help, though time by itself doesn't heal wounds. It's what happens during that time that brings a sense of aliveness once again. There is no easy solution to the complicated and primal grief of losing one's dignity, identity, loved ones, or sense of safety.

When Kateryna speaks to her therapist, her thoughts are rightfully obsessed with terror and worst-case scenarios that prevent her from sleeping. When she says she is resigned, she really means she is feeling hopeless with her current ways of coping.

Most of the time, people come to see mental-health professionals in the aftermath of a tragedy. Yet I often work with people who continue to live in danger—who are still subject to war, human trafficking, or detention, who are trying to survive and not yet in a place of relative safety.

At this very moment, there are innumerable people suffering from active violation and exploitation. And there are even more who, like Kateryna, are experiencing suffering due to not knowing if loved ones are safe or even alive.

In these contexts, many wonder: What can one possibly do to survive the pain of suffering? I've asked myself that question time and time again, especially now, as a clinical consultant to Kateryna's therapist.

Every clinician has a memorable patient who keeps them up at night. Stumped, they search for answers, eager to learn and hone their skills in an inexhaustible curriculum. For many therapists, ambiguous loss is the kind of case that keeps them humble. Together, Kateryna's therapist and I show her how to engage in rituals that help her let go of self-blame and maintain hope during this liminal time.

Ritualize Hope

In the late 2000s, a psychiatrist named James Griffith was rounding with his medical students and residents at the George Washington University Hospital in Washington, DC. With decades of clinical experience behind him, he was accustomed to caring for psychiatric patients who also had chronic illnesses—those with unexplainable pains and fatigue, who were managing heart disease or dealing with the effects of a stroke, who had seizure disorders or recurrent cancers. Managing his patients' helplessness, confusion, and subjective incompetence when they felt they were failing to live up to their own expectations for coping was part of his daily job.

It was common for patients to become distressed. After all, not only did they have the daily stressors of life, they also faced stigma, loss of social status, unemployment, conflicted relationships, pain, and uncertain futures. Demoralized and wanting to return to a previous healthier or more stable life, they often had suicidal impulses or apathy, or gave up on treatment—they were worn out.

Yet what stumped Dr. Griffith more than the resignation of his patients was the resignation of his trainees. Dr. Griffith noticed the effect the patients had on his students, who suffered from an emotional contagion of sorts. Unclear on how to move forward, patients felt unable to survive the present, and this nihilism bled over to trainees, who then doubted their own competence and began to distance themselves from those they were supposed to be caring for.

In response, Dr. Griffith developed what he termed *hope modules*: brief psychotherapeutic interventions to build hope in the face of demoralization. The central premise is that *hope* is a verb. In the most dire of situations, we can use hope as a path forward.

Because hope is something you do, not something you feel. Whether you're physically debilitated or chronically struggling with challenges or uncertainty, hope can help you identify a desire and take a step toward attaining it.

As Dr. Griffith notes, there are four main types of coping that are backed by how the brain works:

(1) Executive function: Using thinking skills to get organized, make plans, stay focused, and solve problems

(2) Relational coping: Connecting with others to feel supported, which helps calm stress by triggering the parts of the brain that respond to empathy

(3) Asserting identity and group belonging: Feeling confident in who you are and having a sense of belonging in a group

(4) Emotion regulation: Managing emotions so they don't over-whelm you

Each of these can be used to ritualize a practice of hope, and everyone will have their own personal ritual. Think of the last time you went through something difficult. How did you respond? What helped you through it? Some have a natural tendency to reach out to friends; others turn to prayer; still others listen to music. It's important to be mindful that what works for you might not work for someone else (please don't tell me to go for a run)!

Ritualizing Natural Ways of Coping

Executive functioning. Kateryna needs a way to find hope. Every morning, she peels herself out of bed and sits at her desk. She writes down two things she wants to focus on for the day and what she'll need to do to accomplish those. Initially, her priorities are focused on agencies to contact and chores to attend to. Dr. Griffith often uses the metaphor of being in a rowboat with alligators nearing—you deal with whichever alligator is closest.

After about a month, she feels more confident in her ability to succeed and creates some internal goals, such as *laugh* and *feel peace*. Her day then revolves around planning an activity in which she is likely to accomplish this. Kateryna's process is what researchers call *shift-and-persist problem-solving.* She's activating the thinking part of the brain by defining a goal and breaking it down, working through what small steps are needed to accomplish the goal.

Yet, as anyone who has tried to lose weight knows, setting a goal and mapping out a plan of action aren't a guarantee of success. Often, self-limiting beliefs too easily sway or sabotage efforts. So we need to pair this goal-oriented thinking with changing attitudes and self-talk. Leaning on this kind of executive functioning helps you to reframe current stressors while at the same time keeping a hopeful eye on the future—you manage the alligators closest to the boat while you're also rowing toward safety.

Relational coping. In the face of upending life events, some people immediately turn to support from those around them. Mirror neurons are at play here. When you engage with another person, a circuit of mirror neurons is activated—brain cells that fire when you act and when you see someone else acting. Mirror-neuron circuits help you emotionally resonate with others, leading to an emotional connection that provides relief if you are going through stress.

Kateryna chose to open her home for a gathering at which she made her daughter's favorite foods. To her surprise, friends and family thanked her, and they continued the ritual monthly. If you've ever helped support a loved one, you know that positive benefits go both ways. The connection allowed loved ones to feel less alone in the ambiguity.

Asserting identity and group belonging. Just as people find comfort by leaning into their tribes, they are also painfully aware of being where they *don't* belong. When life flips you upside down, envy, anger, and resentment toward "the other"—usually those who seem untouched by your suffering—rise to the surface. As Kateryna describes it, "I feel like I'm drowning in an ocean and there are people on their yachts just looking at me while they continue their party." She's not only navigating grief, she's also managing the growing chasm she feels between herself and a world that seems to be moving on without her. The sense of disconnection pulls her further into isolation.

This is the human brain's survival wiring in action. In times of upheaval, the brain activates its social-cognition system, sorting people into categories: *Who's in my group and who's out?* From affiliation to identity, the brain asks, *Who are my people?* and *Where do I belong?*

Yet belonging isn't only about finding a group, it's also about feeling *worthy* of being in one. When Kateryna sees herself as broken or burdensome, shame starts to creep in with a sense that she's not as stable as others, which brings her into an internal exile, corroding her self-respect. Studies show this kind of disconnection from one's identity or place of belonging can deepen isolation and, in darker moments, even fuel suicidal thoughts.

Grief threatened to consume Kateryna until she discovered an organization dedicated to rescuing abducted children and supporting affected families. Through their programs, she connected with other mothers who shared her anguish. They shared stories, offered solace, and found strength in their shared identity as Ukrainian mothers whose children were affected by the war.

Through these connections, Kateryna has reclaimed her identity, becoming not just a grieving mother but a part of a resilient community. Together, the women remind one another they aren't alone and lean on one another for strength; their shared experiences pave a way toward healing.

Emotion regulation. Stress that comes from overwhelm and unpredictability targets the prefrontal cortex, hurting your ability to manage your distress, develop strategies to effectively counter loneliness and agitation, and regulate your anxieties as you wait for something in your life to change. Desperate to clear your mind, you busy yourself with mundane tasks.

Yet calmness can be ritualized. Whether it's engaging in a daily morning meditation, as Kateryna chooses to do, yoga, mindfulness, breathing, exercising, or calling upon a religious or spiritual practice, you can lower the distress that accompanies the instability in your life. Ritualizing these hope practices provides a path forward when hope is hard to sustain. Despair is contagious. And so is hope.

I would be engaging in a form of naive optimism to say that Kateryna is thriving while her kidnapped daughter's life remains ambiguous. What I can say, though, is that Kateryna shows how one can continue in life despite bearing witness to the horrors. Using rituals to scaffold her complex feelings around ambiguity and separation, she's able to act on behalf of her daughter while also finding moments of hope and even aliveness to carry her through.

While narratives and beliefs must be realized through behaviors, behaviors can help inform how you think and feel. Holding on to both desire and doubt is hard. Kateryna may not feel calm, generous, or thankful, but after ritualizing hope, she is able to access those qualities in action. When we use rituals in a space that's neither here nor there, we end up with a little more mastery. Letting go of something we have little power over helps us remember what we can influence—and motivates us to keep going.

Action Tools for Liminal Spaces

A. Define Ambiguity

1. Shift from closure to meaning. When someone disappears from your life, physically or emotionally, you're left with a question mark instead of a period. Ambiguous loss is absence without answers, and it hurts, since humans are wired to crave certainty. When you can't find clarity, choose meaning instead. Redefine *closure*. Ask yourself, *What does peace look like right now?* Aim for integration over resolution and create rituals of meaning.

2. Grieve without permission. There's no standard ritual for this kind of grief. If the world won't validate your pain, validate it yourself. Embrace emotional agility, the ability to hold grief and gratitude at the same time. Flexibility keeps you standing when the ground is shifting. Create your own ritual of release.

3. Replace pathology with possibility. Instability fractures one's sense of self and often creates a cascade of self-blame and shame for not being able to thrive in the moment. Reframe the focus from what's wrong to what's possible to counteract helplessness and support a constructive, future-oriented identity.

B. Ritualize Hope

4. Elicit your individual strengths. Hope comes from the stories we tell ourselves about who we are in the face of suffering. We each have individual ways of coping through hardship. Think of a time when you went through something difficult. How did you get through it? Most coping comes in the form of goal-setting, engaging relationally, asserting group belonging, and regulating emotion.

5. Uncover the core values, spiritual beliefs, or cultural traditions that give meaning. These internal anchors persist when everything else feels uncertain. Serving as a compass during chaos, these can inform rituals to focus on who you care about, what you're looking forward to, and how you envision healing.

6. Activate your communal and relational resources. Instability is hard to manage, but it's even harder when you're at it alone. Knowing you're not alone sustains motivation, even when you don't know the outcome. Strengthen your social ties and reinforce connections to your community and those who add value to your life.

6

Reintegration:
Self-Transformation

In my reintegration to a post-divorce life with two children, I thought the best way to "find myself again" was to resume old hobbies from my single years: organize community fundraisers at local bars, travel for long solo hikes, and attempt kitesurfing again. But they didn't provide the same gratification as they had in the past. It was different. *I* was different.

So much had changed in eight years—I was now a mother of two and had moved across the country. My body had changed; I no longer carried it with the same inviting energy, because people and opportunities now felt like added responsibilities.

One day as I was reading in a café, it dawned on me: This was my life two decades ago. Single and living alone, working out of coffee shops, days scaffolded by yoga practice. Seemingly not much had actually changed.

I'd wanted to move forward by returning to some more "authentic" part of myself, but doing so had brought me to a standstill. I could have jumped into dating again, but I had little interest. Not only had I devoted my life to two children over the past decade, I now understood the hidden narratives that fueled my relationships—and, frankly, I was scared that I wouldn't be able to end the repetition compulsion that underpinned my personal and professional life. I was stuck.

Reentering life after the demise of a relationship, following a traumatic experience, or at the end of a global pandemic causes tension, and many people yearn for a way to calm themselves. How does one move through life after finally putting down a heavy weight they had to carry for so long?

There's something people often get wrong about recovery. The assumption is that when the crisis is over and they're past the survival phase, they'll immediately return to a stable life. If they've experienced anguish in work, love, or play, they think they need to get up, push through, and keep moving toward firm ground. They desperately cling to the familiar and believe that stability is the norm and any interruptions are temporary. The reality is far from that.

I've found that once the chaos ends, the gravity of what's happened starts to sink in—sometimes a week later, other times a year or five years later. The constant stress of survival keeps one preoccupied. It's one reason why I used to focus on the *post*-conflict setting. During a crisis, international aid groups sweep in; they leave one to three years later, after the emergency phase ends. But this is the time when the psychological impact often hits hardest. In a reintegration phase, a second crisis quietly unfolds over months and years. It's this phase that is often harder than anyone ever imagined.

Psychological and disaster research supports this concept of delayed trauma that sneaks up on people long after the crisis has passed. Researchers Sandro Galea and colleagues set out to understand the long-term impacts of Hurricane Katrina, one of the most devastating natural disasters in US history. Their study showed that in the immediate wake of Katrina, people engaged in what disaster psychologists call the *honeymoon phase* of solidarity. People came together, communities rallied, and there was an undeniable sense of solidarity. Hope, purpose, and optimism lifted people's spirits as they leaned on each other.

But something changed. A year later, the numbers looked starkly different. Depression rates doubled and PTSD cases surged. The very people who had seemed to be holding it together were now struggling. Almost one-third of survivors had serious mental distress—

not immediately after the hurricane but in the longer term. This shines a light on a common misconception about crises: Just because people appear to be managing okay now doesn't mean they will be okay in a year.

Why? Galea's team pointed to an unsettling truth: The slow grind over the longer term is where healing is truly tested. Initially, adrenaline builds momentum, a sense that everyone is in this together, with journalists and funds pouring in. But as the months pass, people return to the humdrum of daily life, support systems fray, and reality sets in. The stress hasn't lifted much even though the world has moved on, with the survivors still stuck in the wreckage. That's when the weight of it all finally lands.

The idea that we should focus on mental health and well-being only during a challenging time misses the real danger zone. In the months and years that follow a crisis, the process of reintegration is critical. Grief doesn't just evaporate. As one former child soldier asked rhetorically, "When the war is over, is it ever really over?"

Integrating the Past with Your Present-Day Self

Nina felt a bit unsettled as she drove her children to school one morning near the end of January 2024. The day had started as usual; she'd warmed steamed buns for her kids' breakfast, helped them brush their teeth, and stuffed their backpacks with water bottles and lunch boxes. *Today's a bit warmer than normal,* she told herself, *maybe that's it.*

Nina was born in Vietnam and of Chinese descent; her parents came to the United States as Vietnamese boat refugees. They landed in Monterey Park, California, about seven miles east of downtown Los Angeles. She was thankful to live and raise her family here, and she wasn't alone in that—Monterey Park was listed as one of the top "Ten Best Places in America to Raise a Family" by *Money* magazine. With about 65 percent of its residents of Asian descent, the city was the first in the mainland United States to have a majority of Asian residents. Nina was grateful for the easy access to Hong Kong fusion cafés and Cantonese seafood restaurants and enjoyed hearing the various Chinese dialects that were spoken in the streets.

She was the director of behavioral health at the Chinatown Service Center, and was one of almost two hundred staff across their nine sites in Southern California. With more than fifty years of service, the organization was a well-known part of the community fabric. So why was she feeling so unsettled?

She drove by the Star Ballroom dance studio, now abandoned, the sidewalk strewn with flowers and cards. *Ah, right,* she said to herself. *It's the one-year remembrance of the mass shooting.*

On January 21, 2023, tens of thousands of people gathered for one of Southern California's largest lunar new year celebrations. At night, the Star Ballroom Dance Studio, which usually attracted hundreds of older Asian Americans, hosted a countdown dance party. Wearing their best *qipaos* (high-necked, fitted, vibrant red dresses with elaborate gold embroidery) and *hanfu* (two-piece outfits with long lapels), older Asian American adults shuffled into the ballroom studio, eager to get rid of the old and embrace the new. Many Asian societies celebrate the end of the winter season, during which farmers are less busy and can now enjoy their harvest.

Dancers who had recaptured their youth spun around the floor with the flurry that passed through the studio that night: hundreds of Thai Chinese, Vietnamese Chinese, Taiwanese, and mainland Chinese first-generation immigrants all mingled together to celebrate.

Massaging sore feet and tired from the night, a group of Thai dancers made their way to the parking lot, beaming with the energy of a joyous evening. Exhausted spouses and friends waited in their cars for a few minutes while their companions finished their goodbyes. Then they heard it: gunshots.

At 10:22 P.M., screaming dancers poured out of the studio and fled through the parking lot. A total of forty-two rounds were fired in the dance hall, killing eleven and injuring ten others.

Nina and the staff of the Chinatown Service Center had been integral to the rehabilitation of the community over the past year.

Yet the studio still sat abandoned. The restaurants and shops nearby were back in business, flashing Open signs that most turned their eyes away from. The staff of the Chinatown Service Center knew the community needed healing—but how?

I was sent to Monterey Park to support building a resilience center that would be tasked with restoring dignity and safety to the community. While many wanted to move forward with life and forget about what happened, they were also stumbling in the dark. The community was on edge, worried that another threat could tear away the tenuous sense of stability. The reality of what had happened was an ever-present scent in the air—their lives were both the same and different at once.

A year after the shootings, the community was no longer in crisis mode. For the past year, they had surged in community activism: Offices had reopened, tai chi resumed, and outreach phone calls were made. But this was the critical time when healing was tested. External support had faded. Media attention was gone. The community could resume life as normal—but they weren't feeling normal. In fact, they were feeling disengaged with life, lacking motivation and interest, almost languishing. It turns out that surviving is only part of a crisis. The part we don't talk about enough is how to find your way in a life that no longer looks the same.

Reintegration is harder than most people think. It challenges one's identity. During the crisis, everyone had a clear purpose: First responders managed the victims. Cultural elders provided spiritual guidance. Grandmothers made food for the helpers. But when the crisis ended, the sense of mission disappeared, stripping people of a shared purpose and identity.

Then there's the issue of community support. At the height of a crisis, people step up for each other. Strangers become lifelines. But over time, social connections fade and people are expected to move on. The problem: Instabilities don't work this way. Reintegration isn't like flipping a switch—it's a long, nonlinear, and messy process.

Integrating the past into the present goes beyond acknowledging what's happened. We can use our neurobiology to integrate across time, people, memories, and narratives. There's a top-down vertical integration that opens communication between the cortex (the outer, thinking, rational part of the brain) and the limbic system (the deep, inner, emotional seat of the brain).

Take my post-divorce anklets as an example. I used the anklets as a way to direct my thoughts toward feeling more connected to my children. This top-down approach is in part why therapy works—processing with another helps to connect thoughts and feelings.

Yet longitudinal research shows that the most protective factor post-crisis isn't therapy (although it is helpful!). It's a sense of belonging. Reintegration isn't about returning to a time of stability; it's about a community redefining what's normal, together. Whether through new roles, routines, or narratives, simple rituals can scaffold a process of reintegration across time.

Nina wasn't sure where to begin to address her staff's disengagement and low morale now, a year after the shooting, so she decided a good starting point was what she knew—her community. They supported reintegration into a newly defined world through rituals: a memory wall where people were invited to write messages in a public healing space to rebuild a sense of safety and trust, and a remembrance vigil to gather as a community to share memories among family members of those affected.

But they went on to do something they hadn't thought they could do. They resumed ballroom dancing, now infused with discussions on well-being before each session to strengthen a collective identity. Personal healing became part of a greater collective journey. Harnessing collective support grounded in culture, these ballroom-dance events allowed the community to restore well-being, find meaning through connection, and integrate the individual and collective experiences of the past into their daily lives.

Assimilating what's happened can transform feelings of being shattered and disoriented into actions that create the world you want to see. Psychiatrist Dan Siegel calls this MWE (me plus we), which is the integration of identity from an individual perspective to one that recognizes interconnectedness.

This was the strength of Nina and the Chinatown Service Center, and it's something we can all learn from. Although each person had a unique individual response to the shooting, all were interconnected. Nina was able to use rituals to integrate individual experiences to the wider Monterey Park community, honoring each person's personal differences while reminding people that at their core, their true identity was in togetherness.

I've found that those most able to transform into a life of steadfast confidence are those who can create a through line that incorporates their past and present selves. Think of the banker who never wants to return to the trailer park in which she was raised and the executive who avoids contentious family reunions—the task of integrating the past into the present looms large. People try to bury what happened, but that often leaves them disoriented. Unsettled. Rituals create a sense of connection that helps people reestablish trust, rebuild routines, and adapt to a new version of normal, together.

The Cost of Striving

Layla grew up in a crowded apartment, where the clamor of her siblings and the late-night buzz of Arabic news filled the background. Her parents had never finished high school and spent their days and nights reminding Layla of what they never had: "Education is your only way out."

She believed them. She studied at the kitchen table until midnight, skipped dances and sleepovers, and graduated at the top of her class. Law school was her dream and escape plan. She wanted to be the first in her family to attend college and rewrite the family story of hardship.

But when she made it, success felt lonelier than failure. At her elite law school, she found herself shrinking when classmates spoke about study-abroad trips and private-firm internships. She returned home for all breaks and worked multiple jobs—as a receptionist and a store clerk—to help the family while navigating the quiet resentment of friends who assumed she thought she was above them. Her parents bragged about her to neighbors but Layla didn't know how to talk about the life she was building, as she didn't quite fit in there either.

At times, an achieved "stability" comes at a cost—isolation. Between two worlds, she compartmentalized the cultural bereavement of lost friends, social norms, and attitudes. Caught between obligations and a desire to help loved ones on the one hand and the desire to personally succeed on the other, she was clued in to the forthcoming instability. While she grieved for those she left behind, those same people also grieved for her. The loneliness that resulted from Layla's choosing to leave her past created constant unrest.

This is the hidden cost of striving: It fractures your sense of self, as you do everything to break into a new world, only to feel exiled from both the one you left and the one you've entered. For many first-generation professionals and college graduates, the path to upward mobility comes with emotional tolls few people talk about: guilt, isolation, and the nagging sense that you've traded belonging for achievement.

Layla wasn't sure how to fix this, but one night after a difficult week, her mother sent her a thirty-second voice message about how Layla used to help her fold laundry while reviewing vocabulary words. I asked Layla to turn this into a ritual. Now every Sunday night, Layla and her mother exchange short voice messages—her mother shares a memory of Layla's childhood, and Layla tells her one thing she did that week that she's proud of.

This is more than connection, it's reintegration—reclaiming the idea that her new self doesn't have to cancel out her old one. While the ritual didn't entirely fix her feeling of being split, it gave that feeling form and rhythm to strengthen her identity and emotional continuity.

Psychologists call this a *ritual of integration*—a deliberate act that bridges identity, history, and emotion. Rituals tied to family or cultural heritage have been shown to significantly improve emotional resilience among first-generation students navigating predominantly white, affluent institutions.

What matters isn't the complexity of the ritual but the co-creation and emotional continuity it offers. What's powerful about co-created rituals is that they're rooted in relationship and remind you that you're not becoming someone entirely new, just expanding the definition of who you are.

When we strive, we often picture a finish line, a place where discomfort fades away. But the reality is more complex. Even after you've poured yourself into building a new life, that hard-won future can feel unfamiliar, even destabilizing. Instead of clarity, you're left with a quieter kind of disorientation: the ache of arriving somewhere you're not sure you belong. In those moments, co-created rituals, especially with people who know where you've come from, can become bridges to ground you in both who you were and who you're becoming.

Collective Rituals

Sierra Leone is a country defined by a deep sense of community and vibrant culture—if you aren't a child soldier. For Binta, it was a battlefield. In her home in Sierra Leone, the twenty-four-year-old shows her hospitality by pouring me tea during an interview I'm conducting on healing practices of former child soldiers.

Binta didn't acquire good graces from her mother. She mastered them from her commander. Had you met her a decade ago, you'd likely have screamed in terror and run in the opposite direction. At age ten, Binta was abducted during a village attack and forced into child soldiering during the eleven-year civil war over political corruption, economic inequality, and control over diamond resources. In 1991, a rebel group launched an invasion from neighboring Liberia, initiating a brutal civil war that involved widespread atrocities, including the abduction of children.

If you think it couldn't get worse, it did. After they abducted the children, officers forced them to maim, sexually assault, and steal from their own family and community members, leaving the children no choice but to return to their abductors.

The media tends to focus on the young boys who were forced to kill and pillage; however, girls were also used as child soldiers. When the fighting finally ended, many boys entered demobilization camps for rehabilitation and reintegration into society. But the girls were forgotten.

Binta was one of those girls. Within two days of her abduction, she was sexually assaulted. After the first week, commanders decided that she would become a fighter and began her training. Binta recalls: "They worked us before dawn and made us run the bush paths carrying bags of rice and ammunition. If anyone fell, they beat all of us. They rubbed powder into small cuts on our arms and said it would make us brave."

The purpose of this training was to instill fear in the children to ensure compliance as well as to shift them from their "civilian" morals to "rebel" ones. Binta was forced to torture and kill some of her peer abductees. "I really missed my family and wanted my old life back. But to survive, I couldn't think like that anymore. I had to just change my thinking because I never knew what was going to happen to me," she recalls.

While other girls were designated as "wives" for various soldiers, Binta wasn't assigned to anyone. Rather, she was available to everyone. Quickly, she realized that the key to survival was to let go of a dream of stability and focus on how to stay alive each day.

After a brief peace agreement in 1999 failed to stop the fighting, the disarmament of the remaining rebel forces in early 2002 finally brought the war to a close. Both the rebel groups and government forces had recruited child soldiers. While the boys in Binta's armed group were given cash allowances as part of a demobilization package, she got nothing even though she was impregnated by her chief, who later chose to keep her.

By the age of twenty-one, she'd witnessed the murder of blood relatives and the burning of her home, suffered repeated sexual violations by multiple men, and had given birth to a son who was taken from her. Yet what almost ended Binta wasn't the war. It was the loss of a place of belonging *after* the war.

Although she was aware that her family perceived her to be a burden, a part of her still quietly dreamed of being released into the open arms, validation, and love of family and community. But a sense of stability remained beyond her grasp.

While her parents welcomed their daughter home, they also feared her. The community openly rejected her, for she'd been sexually violated—a taboo in their village—and was seen as part of the armed group that violated their community. So while she was reunited with her closest family members, she was far from reintegrated. Withdrawn, dwelling on her losses, staring at the wall at night, and picking at her food, she was tormented by anger toward the world and herself.

Limits to Self-Reliance

When people's lives are upended, they commonly focus on self-regulation strategies such as breathing, walking away, and counting to ten. Yet a total reliance on regulating emotions doesn't work. Humans have evolved to constantly regulate emotions and develop their sense of self and identity through communities, family, and peers—through relationships.

But where does that leave Binta, who stole from, assaulted, and burned the homes of the people in that very community? "My neighbors told me I'm a monster," she says. "I came back to my home village and people remembered what I'd done." Though starved for connection, she resigned herself to being invisible.

Until she was cleansed. The village organized, paid for, and performed a body-purification ritual as a sign of care—a gesture of reconciliation and healing. Traditional healers, gentle with touch and soft with compassion, invoked the powers of the ancestral spirits to help cleanse and purify her body.

To symbolically seal her demons out, the healer cleansed her body of the accumulated "dirt" of the past with herbal infusions. She was then reintroduced to the village and its chief, and they all shared a ceremonial meal with traditional beer to show acceptance. After singing, dancing, and feasting, Binta was accepted. The community felt like a safe place for Binta again, a little less hypervigilant and a little more welcoming.

Binta remains aware of the precariousness of life; it's imprinted on her soul. While others were shocked when political upheaval struck again after a period of stability, she was relatively calm. "I had to learn to live without knowing where to eat, or whether I would be hit, or worse."

Through the purification ritual, she now pairs her true suffering and hardship with adaptation and belonging. Binta ultimately gained another kind of certainty: trust and confidence in herself. Community reconciliation led to her own transformation.

Rituals influence your individual, subjective sense of yourself. As reflections of the history and communities that create them, they blend what you believe, what you feel, even how you feel into the larger communal social order. Serving an important social function, rituals reliably mark your membership, show your commitment, and foster cohesion within a group. Witnessing a quinceañera or a confirmation before having one's own teaches which social norms are most important to the group.

Rituals can therefore connect your inner experience (your thoughts, feelings, and behaviors) to your outer social experiences (your relationships, culture, and traditions) to foster self-transformation.

At the same time, the very communities and relationships that are there to support you can also become a source of stress. Binta's rituals restored her place of belonging within the community—something we all desperately need at times. Social cohesion is commonly thought to maintain peace, security, and safety. But at what expense?

While the purification ritual restored Binta's membership in her community, the practice also restored the social expectations of her as a submissive woman in comparison to her male counterparts. Meaning that rituals aren't always risk-free. Complex and dynamic, some rituals can inadvertently reinforce social norms that undermine one's well-being. To ease the conflict between respecting your own individual needs and upholding local traditions or norms, you need to be mindful of which rituals you're maintaining or developing.

Herein lies the complexity of the interplay between our individual and cultural rituals, similar to our narratives. When a collective ritual conflicts with your personal values, you face a choice: conform, resist, or find a path that honors your identity and community relationships.

People encounter this conflict between personal values and collective rituals all the time: the workplace happy hours or heavy drinking rituals that may go against your personal value of abstaining for various health, religious, or personal reasons; patriarchal wedding traditions that can be at odds for those with feminist beliefs; reciting the pledge of allegiance at school, sports events, or activities when it contains messages that counter your individual beliefs; even holiday gift-giving that may go against your personal values of avoiding material excess.

Rituals aren't just routines; they're psychological anchors that help you make sense of who you are and where you belong. Whether you're a soldier reintegrating into civilian society after returning from active combat or a mom returning home to be with the kids after a busy day at work, rituals can ease the transition. Individually, rituals are mirrors for your values, reinforcing what matters most—whether it's a morning meditation to cultivate awareness or a personal tradition of sending thank-you notes to ground yourself in gratitude. Collectively, they create a shared expression of meaning, strengthening social bonds and signaling belonging.

Attending to your personal and collective rituals paves a path toward self-transformation as you evaluate your life, acknowledge uncomfortable feelings, and identify dreams and planned achievement for the time ahead. Separation, loss, and reintegration can orient you to what really matters, and rituals can boost you beyond the rhythm and routine of daily ennui.

Time speeds up and hope awakens. During those times when your sense of self is so upended by instability that you can't think your way through the storm, you can be reminded that your behaviors can guide you back to who you want to be in ways that knowledge alone cannot.

Action Tools for Reintegration

A. Reframe *Normal* as Something to Rebuild, Not Return To

1. Honor the invisible aftermath. The most difficult phase of recovery often begins when the crisis ends. Rituals give structure to this reintegration to a new normal; they help people feel seen, connected, and empowered to move forward together. Collective healing means we co-author a new normal rather than pretending to resume the old one. Host a milestone gathering focused on growth, not just grief, and invite people to share what's changed in them. Normalize long-term support with monthly check-ins or shared walks.

2. Design rituals that integrate the experience, not erase it. Rituals aren't about forgetting; they're about making meaning. Rather than bypassing pain, they give us a safe space to carry it forward. Make meaning tangible by creating something lasting, like a bench by a tree or a piece of art, that marks the journey through the experience, not just the event itself. Facilitate spaces where people can share not just what happened but what it taught them.

B. Integrate Identities During Transition

3. Treat identity tension as a space for growth. When you're caught between two worlds, rituals give you a way to carry both. They provide structure, connection, and identity continuity. Use visual anchors and keep photos and mementos from your past visible in your current environment.

4. Preserve micro-traditions. Small rituals carry big meaning. Micro-traditions, like a favorite meal, shared practice, or weekly call, anchor you to your identity and remind you where you come from, even in unfamiliar environments. Preserving familiar practices and co-creating rituals to bind you to your relationships in new contexts helps you reduce cultural dissonance, offering emotional scaffolding during transitions.

C. Adapt Collective Rituals When Needed

5. Name the dissonance when rituals feel misaligned. Collective rituals can bring people together, but they can leave you feeling more isolated if they ignore complexity. The key is to engage and personalize through honest reflection. After engaging in a ritual, consider what felt real and what felt performative. Design your own parallel ritual or celebrate privately first.

6. Honor the intention by shifting the expression. Collective rituals often serve a valuable purpose of connection, closure, or celebration. By staying engaged and adjusting how you participate, you can preserve the spirit of the ritual while aligning it with your own values and experiences. Ask yourself, *What is this ritual trying to represent?* If the group practice feels off, add a personal gesture that brings it closer to your truth. Participate with presence but allow yourself to adapt or opt out of specific parts if needed.

PART III

PURPOSE

Plum blossoms (매실, *meshil*, in Korean; 梅, *mei*, in Chinese; 梅, *ume*, in Japanese): A symbol of winter, plum blossoms bloom vibrantly in the snow with a subtle fragrance that lasts even at the coldest times of the year. In Asian art, they symbolize perseverance, hope, virtue, and the transitoriness of life.

I couldn't understand at first why I was still feeling so untethered. It was exactly one year after the divorce and I had reorganized and recentered. As the year progressed, the gut-wrenching pain of not seeing my children every other weekend stung a little less as paralysis gave way to growth. Belly-aching laughter and weekend trips with the kids resumed; playdates restarted; my focus returned to my work and activities that nourished me. Quick to believe the worst was behind us, I sighed with relief. We were on stable ground.

The whiplash of relief stung, though, when the attic fan in my house suddenly sparked into flames on the one-year anniversary of my divorce. I watched from the front yard as smoke engulfed the top of my home. Five minutes after I'd called emergency services, blaring engines quieted the crowd that had gathered across the street. Firefighters scrambled up the hook and ladder toward billowing smoke escaping through the roof.

In a matter of two hours, half the home collapsed. Toy monster trucks and baby dolls smothered in smoke. Stuffies and lovies hid microscopic shards of fiberglass. The following months were a blur of fire-mitigation crews conducting smoke mapping, water tracing, dwelling measurements, inventory identification, and demolition. My own work paused as I scrambled for twelve-month housing.

Loved ones tried to infuse hope: "Life will be a lot more stable a year from now." "Just get through this and you'll be back on track." I wanted to believe this but couldn't. Perhaps life would be stable in a year—or maybe another life event would pummel me again. Before the fire, there had been a job change, a pandemic, then a divorce, so I was no stranger to the overwhelm, anxiety, and fury that is a normal and natural response to major disruptions.

Setting daily priorities of action and goals became a source of survival. Yet at the end of each day, I bumbled listlessly, despite accomplishing my objectives. Organizing my life around goals usually puts me on solid ground, so this sense of listlessness in existence was new. Aside from feeling gratitude for friends and neighbors who'd stepped up to support, I found little relevance in life. Days blurred together.

Major instabilities don't have much regard for anyone's schedule. But I didn't have much regard for this particular upheaval. I wanted to stall and place the hourglass on its side. I was developing and working on projects with people around the world, many of whom were living in much worse conditions than I was. Ukrainian colleagues sent me a thinking-of-you card between their air strikes and bombings; my Tigrayan colleague sent me condolences: *I'm so sorry, my house also burned down from a drone strike. I know what it's like.* My house fire seemed like an inconvenient coffee spill in comparison.

Trying to stay afloat, I set and accomplished more goals—work would be my lifeboat for now to take me to solid ground. With so many transitions, I just wanted something to have control over. But as neuroscience predicted I would when stressed, I went back to old habits: I binged on drama series, aimlessly popped Korean snacks in my mouth, and hid from friends. Hope was depleting. I collapsed on the floor and lay in the darkness. And then I remembered: *I have to feed the bunny.*

As I changed her hay and then crossed off the twelfth item on my to-do list, I reflected on my productive lassitude, the trouble I was having clearing my mind and finding a sense of grounding. *Of course,* I thought. *I don't have a purpose.*

I have never felt more lost and insecure than I did the year of disruptions in my family, house, and career. With my sense of security upended, I reflected on life thus far—what progress had I actually made? I thought I had moved up in the world—I'd gone to Ivy League schools, married, had two kids, bought a home in a safe neighborhood, and was on the top rung of the career ladder. I had met all my goals. Yet life, quite literally, went up in flames.

Having prestigious jobs and holding fancy titles and initials after my name didn't protect me from major disruptions, and some relationships actually became the problem. What was worse, transition points in both career and connections were especially painful because they came at a time when I was most unsure of myself and yet people wanted to see me at the top of my game.

Throughout the days I worked remotely in a rented apartment, my thoughts took me to the heart of the matter: *What am I doing with my life?*

I know I'm not alone in coping through overworking and rethinking my life's purpose after a major disruption. Many people seek my help during a path of transition. Whether it's entering college, sliding into the middle of one's career, adjusting to retirement, or changing jobs or relationships, all of us can wake up one day and find ourselves experiencing the instability of self-doubt and lack of direction.

Most people don't slow down, because they're striving for some kind of stability and control. With the threat of loss so hard to bear, they doggedly continue, wanting to get to solid ground. After the job loss, the breakup, or the loss of a loved one, how do we move through the next stages—six months later, a year later? What helps us decide what we should be working on next or whom to invite into our circle of relationships?

Most often, our compass points toward stability. But if our goals are driven by a motivation for stability, short-term ease can quickly give way to long-term confusion as we attach ourselves to positions or people who don't value us or lead us down a path of demise. Grasping what is familiar or known may help us quickly define goals, as that gives an easy path of action, but that isn't always in our best interests.

But there's a difference between being driven and having a purpose. Plenty of people are driven toward accomplishing goals, but I've found that once they're attained, the self-discipline required to reach them starts to relax. That allows the opening for the self-care needed to understand what matters most. *What should I do? How can I be useful? Where should I invest my time and resources?*

Goals are the *what*—they give your efforts direction. Objectives are the *how*—they break the work into manageable steps. But the *why*? That's purpose, and too often it's left out. High achievers are great at tackling objectives and checking boxes. But often, they lose sight of the goal, and they rarely stop to ask why it matters. Ironically, the most driven people sometimes forget what's driving them. Yet being accomplished doesn't spare you from life's instabilities. When purpose is missing, success feels empty and struggle feels like you're just getting by. The difference lies between living with meaning and simply making it through.

So our narratives and rituals work in concert with one more element to help us get through the hard times, regardless of culture or context: having a meaningful existence. While the definition of that varies by individual, many scholars agree that the best way to develop a meaningful existence is to create a feeling that one's life makes sense, have clear and satisfying long-term goals, and develop a belief that one matters in the world. Meaning, mastery, and mattering—those are the tools available to you to embrace the instability in your life with a sense of competence and groundedness.

7

Beyond Goals: Coherence

On the last day of January, Kim received a metaphorical wake-up call that made her question her life. She sat slumped on the floor next to her desk, unable to remember where she was or what she was doing. Her last memory was staring at her office computer, her eyes glazed over, zoning out at the end of the workday. Kim had spent multiple years traveling and managing difficult personalities, and her executive career was driven by a seemingly endless list of goals to accomplish: build a massive portfolio, spearhead global strategy, manage a several-hundred-million-dollar budget. All of these were stepping-stones to the ultimate goal: to get promoted to vice president. Which she had, one week prior.

Kim was often called a powerhouse. In high school, she was voted most likely to succeed. In college, she was editor of the newspaper and made all the honor rolls. Recruited straight after college, she joined a Fortune 500 company and leveled up not once but four times over a decade. With an eye to be president of the company, she was truly unstoppable.

Until housekeeping staff found her passed out underneath her desk, an empty liquor bottle next to her.

A common misconception in our society is that career success brings life fulfillment and stability. From the time children can speak, sometimes even before, they're asked, "What do you want to be when you grow up?" Any junior or senior in high school will tell you that one of their most feared questions is "What will you study in college?" After college, it's "What will you do after graduation?" To hold ourselves steady, we plan out our lives not just a year from now, but sometimes a decade down the line. Kim always had goals at the top of her mind, most of the time not giving herself the emotional space to ask why she wanted them.

The problem was, now she had little desire to work on anything. For the past few years, Kim had disliked her job, building to apathy and loss of respect toward work and those around her. Increasingly, her daily activities felt meaningless and rote. She felt undervalued and at odds with company culture.

Now here she was, feeling trapped with golden handcuffs: She had been promoted to vice president—achieved her dream. But at what cost? She had made it to the top, but once she made it, she wondered, *What am I doing here?*

It's not unusual for people to come to my office in inner turmoil after achieving their goals. Whether it's finally earning that title or selling one's company, many high achievers find a way to minimize their success and continually move goals just out of reach—until the top no longer has appeal.

Accomplishing what we set out to do is an important part of feeling competent, but the autopilot nature of hitting a goal and moving to the next can ultimately leave someone feeling untethered and lost.

Which is what brings Kim into my office after I led a strategic resilience program for senior leaders at her technology company. She realized that while she was skilled at guiding her team through change, she had overlooked her own capacity to navigate it.

Kim had reached all her goals: She worked hard with a focus on a lucrative, prestigious career with a reputable brand, owned a high-rise apartment in San Francisco, and had the kind of schedule that left little room for second-guessing.

But something felt deeply off. Every morning, she'd look in the mirror and try to reconcile the ambitious career-driven executive with the creeping sense that she was living someone else's life.

"I don't know what's wrong with me; maybe I'm depressed. This was my dream to make it to the top." Before she allows herself to consider alternative explanations, she sighs. "I've always had stability. Now I'm floundering. I don't even know if another job would be better." Inertia aside, Kim resigns herself to dissatisfaction.

The problem isn't burnout; it's deeper than that. Without the title, long hours, and external validation, she isn't sure who she is. Family and friends assured her: *Don't worry, you'll find yourself.* But the more she searches, the more lost she feels.

We often believe that it's the negative transitions that make us question who we are and why we're alive. It's true that instability leads us to reflect on what matters most and how we want to live. Many people find their calling after experiencing hardship in a reactive process after a traumatic event or the loss of a loved one.

But as I've seen in many burned-out professionals, sometimes people reach existential distress *because* they've accomplished their goals; they're aimlessly drifting when essential parts of life are in order. The majority of my patients are marginally content with their lives and yearn for more—they crave a purpose.

Questions around one's purpose in life often come during times of transition: *What am I doing with my life, and why?* For many, the internal craving for more is constantly suppressed with whispers of *Be thankful for what you have* or *Who do you think you are to want more?* Without an underlying purpose, people flail with a sense of insecurity.

Goal Habits

A goal habit is remarkably easy to fall into. We all engage in regular checklists of tasks and busywork, most of the time oblivious as to why we're investing our energy in them. The goal to complete a triathlon or earn the next promotion at a company is so socially approved and impressive-sounding that you convince yourself it's what you really want. If you aren't fully motivated, you tell yourself you're just lazy or there's something wrong with you.

Too often, we mistake goals for purpose. Current consensus defines *purpose* as a "generalized intention to accomplish something personally meaningful that also engages productively with the larger world." Accomplishing a goal may help you feel proud and secure in the moment, but studies show how fleeting these emotions are. Give it a couple of days and often you're right back to searching for something more, asking yourself, *What's next?* Earning good grades or attaining a certain job title is a means to an end, not an end in itself. Goals focus on an intention to gain something one doesn't yet have, but purpose is always within reach.

As a highly competent and driven person, Kim has organized her life around achieving goals and she accomplishes what she sets her mind to. But this feeling of control and competence doesn't align with her sense of meaning or mastery. Her relatively persistent dissatisfaction was silenced at times, but it always found a way to resurface.

She lacks a sense of coherence—how aligned the world is in relation to what makes sense to her. We have coherence in our lives when our thoughts, feelings, and behaviors are interconnected and resonant in some meaningful way. Arguments abound between Kim and her husband around finances, chores, and family dynamics. That's not uncommon.

Feeling out of control can spark a pull to control others: children, partners, friends, coworkers, and family members. Instead of looking within and sitting with difficult questions, you might feel it's better to scratch that itch in a different way: by solving other people's problems—even if they don't see their situations as problematic.

As soon as you have a tingle of questioning your stable life, you bounce onto whether your children are in the right school, if your partner is doing her share of household chores, or if your colleague really deserved to get that promotion. It's easier to fixate on how others can improve than to look inward to do the intimidating work of challenging your inner narratives.

Whether you've reached the top or are lamenting your reality, if you can't figure out where you're headed and how to get there, rest assured that you can cultivate your purpose to scaffold goals, guide next steps, and embrace the hard knocks likely to come. Having a purpose in life helps give it direction, like a compass to help direct you out of the forest when you're lost after a storm. But in order to lean into your purpose with coherence, you first need to know who you are.

Who Are You?

For all of Western history, the question *Who am I?* has plagued people after major setbacks. By way of retreats, astrology, and self-help books, people strive to find the "authentic" self—an unchanging core waiting to be reclaimed. But is that the most helpful way to think of it?

Who you are at your core isn't static; you aren't the same person now as you were a decade or two ago. Research in developmental psychology shows that personalities continue to evolve throughout our lives, not just during adolescence. Values, beliefs, and priorities all shift based on the collection of experiences and emotions that you've held. As your narratives and memories are constantly evolving, so, too, is who you know yourself to be. The notion of a stable, fixed, truly "authentic" self needs to give way to the awareness that you are always shaping and being shaped by contexts around you.

Identifying one's purpose first requires embracing the instability of your "authentic" self—the more you cling to the notion of some true self that you need to uncover, the harder it is to adapt to challenges.

Sociologists such as Erving Goffman argue that identity is a performance—we all wear different masks in different contexts. When I visit family in Korea, I am a helpful, acquiescent family member. When I'm home with my children, I'm a playful, affectionate mother. With friends, I'm direct and honest, as I expect them to be. When I'm teaching or training students, I'm a professional, encouraging professor. Different masks, different contexts. All authentically me.

Anthropologists studying indigenous societies have shown that social roles and community interactions do more to define who one is than solitary introspection. In many parts of the world, personhood isn't about discovering who you are but about becoming who you are through others.

While I was preparing a cognitive-behavioral therapy (CBT) evaluation in rural East Africa to determine whether CBT was effective in lowering rates of depression in a war-affected community, I met a woman who was deeply respected in her village. She was well regarded because of how she showed up for others. When I asked her what CBT meant to her, she didn't speak about personal transformation or inner breakthroughs. Instead, she said, "It helps me be more patient with my son. It makes me more useful in community meetings."

Her identity wasn't defined in isolation but in how well she fulfilled the roles important to her—as a mother, neighbor, and leader. Even casual conversations reflected this. If I asked people there, "How are you?" the response would often reference their responsibilities: "I'm not good because I don't have enough to buy school uniforms for my kids" or "We're good because the drought is over and we have crops again." Emotional well-being was rarely articulated as a private state.

Counterintuitively, in order to answer *Who am I?*, ask yourself, *Who am I with respect to others?* Because there's something that many of us get wrong—we think we need solitary introspection with a navel-gazing examination of ourselves, but we learn the most about ourselves from our engagements with others.

For Kim, who had reached the top, only to discover how empty success felt, this lesson would come to life in an unexpected way. After returning to work from a winter-break trip to her childhood home, she received a phone call: Her best friend almost died. This wasn't your ordinary friendship. It was the kind that spanned decades and felt like family. Kim and Lily grew up sharing lunches, secret notes, and heartbreak, all woven into each other's stories since childhood. Their bond was a steady current of love, sustained by weekly calls and late-night confessions that kept them anchored to one another.

Then, one ordinary weekend, everything changed. On a solo hike, Lily lost her footing on a remote trail and was left with a severe concussion and multiple fractures. News of Lily's near-fatal accident felt like a punch in the gut. She received the call during a meeting and spent the rest of the day drinking behind her closed office door.

A month later, as she sits across from me in therapy, she sighs. "Work is up in the air, and now, with this thing with Lily, life just feels so unsteady. I don't know what to do." Although she often tells herself she doesn't know what to do, I believe she does know. Most of the time in therapy, I think my role is to walk next to people trying to get from one side of a forest to the other. Although they tell themselves they aren't sure where their destination is or how to get there, I think they do know—my job is to help clear out the brush in the way.

I ask Kim to tell me what happened with Lily. "Of course I flew out immediately—took a leave from work to stay for a few weeks. I bathed her, managed her meds, and sat with her through the night. It was a lot."

I nod. "What was that like for you, being in that role?"

"Actually, it wasn't as exhausting as one would think. I felt calm." She pauses, almost startled by her own clarity. "It felt right to be there." Kim's voice begins to change as tension is replaced by awareness. "It reminded me of who I am at my best," she says. "Someone who shows up and supports people when they fall apart. I'd forgotten that part of myself and don't want to lose it again. When I die, I want people to say I had a grounded presence that made them feel supported."

In caring for her best friend, Kim had reconnected with a part of herself that had always been there: the grounded, reliable core that made her feel whole. For the first time in years, her life and her values were finally in sync.

I sit, envious of and excited for Kim, and try to extend this awakening for as long as possible. There's a Buddhist term for this kind of epiphany: *satori,* a sudden, deep illumination into life. Epiphanies or flashes of insight, these brief moments offer windows for life changes. Time feels like it's stopping as the ego drops and clarity presents itself.

Most of the time, people experience these moments of illumination and let them pass. If you do that, you miss an opportunity to enact what you know to be true—to carry and direct yourself in ways that align with who you know or want yourself to be.

I encourage Kim to expand her window of illumination. Through caring for her best friend, she's come to understand that who people are isn't hidden inside waiting to be discovered but is continuously shaped by how they show up for others and allow others to show up for them.

While she still feels bored with her role at work, she isn't looking to quit her career as much as reorient it. In meetings, she finds herself listening more and speaking less from a quieter kind of knowing. Her imagined future isn't about titles but about who she will be in the lives of others: a mentor, collaborator, friend. She found her purpose not in a singular focus on an "authentic self" but by anchoring herself in roles and webs of relationships that matter.

Rather than thinking of purpose as emerging from a fixed core self, I think of it more as an alignment—when your actions, words, and values have coherence. If you're feeling unrooted by not knowing who you are, that's not necessarily a bad thing. It's a good starting point to embrace. Your past doesn't define you—the meaning and narratives you derive from it do. You can shift the focus from searching for a preexisting identity to expanding those moments of illumination that help you craft a meaningful life and build more integrity between what you believe in and how you live.

Unveiling the Mask

For most of us, however, there are road blocks to expressing who we believe ourselves to be. There are times and situations in which who people are is perceived as threatening or disturbing, so they downplay aspects of their identity or personality in order to conform or make others comfortable.

A woman executive is told she's "too assertive." A gay physician hears he should "tone *it* down." A girlfriend is labeled "too emotional." Over time, many people—whether in boardrooms, break rooms, or living rooms—learn to edit themselves as they soften their tone, awkwardly laugh at condescending remarks, or strategically downplay their ambitions. As law professor Kenji Yoshino states, masking isn't always a conscious decision; sometimes it's a learned survival skill.

Masking like this comes at a cost. Research shows that when people hide core parts of their identity, stress rises, job satisfaction drops, and cognitive performance suffers. When authenticity is punished, people pull back—not only in who they are but in what they contribute. The result? Organizations, communities, and relationships lose out on the ideas, energy, and impact unlocked by someone's full potential.

Yet, in many cases, masking functions as an essential tool for navigating environments where being seen fully can invite harm. From the immigrant working in a country with anti-Muslim sentiment to the man with autism encouraged to mask his sensory sensitivities to maintain friendships and professionally succeed, covering certain aspects of oneself can provide temporary protection. People are then left in a moral quandary: How much do they contort themselves in order to open doors of opportunity and navigate systems that aren't yet designed for their full inclusion?

What looks like self-betrayal on the surface can sometimes be a strategic act of self-preservation and even a clue to what people care about most. Masking doesn't always have to be about hiding who you are; it can also reveal what matters most to you. You can mask out of fear and care. You can modulate your tone, suppress frustration, or adjust your behavior not only to fit in but to protect others by preserving relationships, maintaining harmony, and showing empathy.

So the real question isn't whether we hide parts of ourselves, since we all do. It's in understanding *why* we hide certain parts of ourselves and whether we have the freedom to take off the mask.

Psychological safety is what allows people to reveal themselves without fear of judgment or punishment. The solution isn't forcing people to unmask at all times; it's creating environments where they don't have to mask in the first place. The danger is when masking is so ingrained that people no longer feel they have the option to be their full selves.

Chronic masking can lead to burnout and disconnection, but you can choose to make masking intentional by tying it to purpose, which gives masking context. You aren't pretending; you're prioritizing. You can opt for less erasing and more conscious choosing of which parts of yourself to spotlight for the sake of something bigger than yourself.

In the end, hiding doesn't just shrink a person—it shrinks the room they're in. When people spend more energy managing perceptions than engaging in meaningful work or relationships, everyone pays a price. The antidote is to create spaces where belonging and authenticity aren't in conflict, so people can bring their full capacity to the table. To get there, we need to understand not only who we are but who we want to be for the people and communities around us—shifting the question from "Am I being fully authentic right now?" to "Am I being true to the kind of person I want to be *for others?*"

Who Do You Want to Be?

Daphne shielded her eyes from the sun she hadn't seen in five months. Her stomach ached from being struck by a black rubber rod; her shins throbbed with fresh boot imprints. Wearing only her underwear and a torn shirt, she tried to cover her bruised body to hide it from the guards' gaze as they released her from detention. In a matter of minutes, her father drove up, gave her a passport with her new name, and kissed her goodbye for good. Her crime? Selling bracelets.

As a young girl, Daphne radiated a confident presence wherever she went. She could always charm her father into buying her a Kit Kat bar after school. She often sang proudly and wildly, and she had no difficulty getting up to talk in front of her class.

But in her community, she posed a problem: She spoke English only. Ordinarily that wouldn't be an issue in school. However, her family belonged to an English-speaking minority group in the mostly Francophone country of Cameroon. And these weren't ordinary times: Predominantly English-speaking citizens supported the Social Democratic Front, the main political opposition party to the ruling Cameroon People's Democratic Movement.

One of seven siblings, Daphne was always worried about the safety of her family. Government officials had beaten one brother outside a political protest, harassed her sister every day at work, and interrogated and detained yet another brother at the market. None of them were members of a political party.

When the family urged Daphne to stay inside their home for safety, the seventeen-year-old insisted on traveling. She was laser-focused on earning enough money to help the family leave the country. Her quest: safety. She took off across the border, seeking new opportunities and ways to earn money. In a neighboring country, she purchased cocoa, coffee, and beads to sell back home. She soon expanded into designing and selling jewelry to churches and schools.

On a day she now regrets, Daphne met a friend for tea. The Social Democratic Front was planning a celebration the following month. "I bet if you made stickers, buttons, and bracelets for the party, you'd make a lot of money—they'd sell fast!" her friend said, beaming. Worried about her own safety, Daphne had always stayed clear of politics. But this could be lucrative; she could make enough to help her family move away from this troubled place.

So Daphne hustled. She designed simple bracelets and other swag in white and green and lugged them to the party, bringing along some coffee to sell as well. It worked—she could barely keep up with the demand. There was a problem, though: This wasn't really a party. It was a rally to organize street demonstrations in Douala, Cameroon's largest city and main port.

The turmoil that followed far exceeded the Social Democratic Front's planned agenda. For five days in February 2008, the country teetered on the brink of collapse. A strike by taxi drivers who opposed increased fuel prices and poor working conditions quickly gave way to rioting around presidential term limits, ethnic and regional strife, political and economic corruption, chronic unemployment, and social and urban blight.

Disaffected youth banded together to loot and vandalize in the major cities of Douala, Yaoundé, and Bamenda. The unrest that February touched on Cameroon's many flashpoints, leaving an estimated one hundred people dead and more than two thousand arrested in Douala alone.

A couple of days after the violent outbreaks, men from the gendarmerie arrived at Daphne's door and requested an interview. When she asked why, she was slapped across the face; the officers grabbed her, shoved her into their van, and drove away before her family returned home. She didn't see them for more than five months as she endured beatings and repeated assaults, humiliation, and sexual violence—all for selling bracelets at a political rally, which led police to assume she was a political dissident.

Though she was eventually released from captivity, the nightmare didn't end. She had to report to the detention center for daily check-ins where she endured degrading humiliation that reminded her she wasn't truly free. Desperate, her father reached out to his estranged brother. Her uncle agreed to help. Five weeks later, she had a plane ticket to the United States in hand.

She landed in an airport in Virginia seven months before I met her. Paralyzed with fear and confusion, she sat on an airport bench for four hours. By a stroke of luck, a kind woman saw the palpable fear in her eyes and asked if she was okay. Daphne possessed neither money nor belongings, but soon she had her first friend. Together, they contacted a local refugee resettlement agency that helped with immediate housing.

Minefields in the Heart

Daphne was confused about how to move forward in a world without her family and fearful for their safety, and was referred to me while she awaited her asylum hearing. She now comes to my office with a sense of resignation. She's been sitting with emotional turmoil for so long, she is beyond desperation, which has an element of hope to it. Apathy and overwhelm collapse her sense of being. Daphne allows only a select few to try to help her, in part because she doesn't believe anyone has the desire or ability to.

Aware of her dark past, I ask her where she would like to start. Tears, hand-wringing, and eyes that dart around the room communicate the unspeakable suffering she's carrying. Daphne longs for her family, for a sense of belonging and motivation to engage in the world. Nostalgic memories flood her mind: playing a trick on her friend at school, curling up in bed with her sister and reading at night, the long conversations she had with her mother as she did her hair. "The ground is moving under me," she tells me.

Oceans away from those who give her a sense of self, Daphne falls into an inner attack: She reprimands herself for not doing more. She pines for a past time when she felt confident, vibrant, and relaxed. Adding to her suffering is a belief that she isn't responding as she should—as if there's a right way to suffer. Nearly constantly, she tells herself, *Get up! Do something! Rise above!* Accompanied by perpetual self-blame, she languishes unmoving in a dimly lit room.

Quickly filling the time with anything to occupy her thoughts, she eats too much, sleeps too much, drinks too much. She strains to focus on anything in her daily life except the next call with loved ones far away, barely speaking to anyone else. Yearning to meet her perceived obligation to her family and anxiety-stricken, she gives in to suffering.

My role as a psychiatrist is often to quietly watch the fires in the shadows long after the wars have died down, to listen to and bear witness to stories and struggles, giving voice to my patients' pain. I have to untangle what is chronic versus situational, determine what might have ignited the suffering, and find a way to create space for change.

"I feel like I'm walking on a minefield. One day I can be okay, but then suddenly I come across something and it all explodes. I get so angry and don't know why. I have no purpose in life." For reasons researchers are still struggling to understand, many people turn their pain inward, and Daphne is no different. Nearly constantly, she asks herself, *What is wrong with me?*

From Self-Regulation to Co-Regulation

As a witness to her deepest moral struggles, I validate Daphne's pain. Her trauma speaks without words through her downward gaze, sweaty palms, and trembling legs. Humiliation, resignation, shame, and fear surface in my office in all forms. Silence is welcome in our conversations—the difference between being *silent* and being *silenced* is in who has control. Paradoxically, Daphne's silence is a loud cry for help.

The human species has evolved to heal through relationships. Humans are born depending on others to help regulate their emotions—infants look to others to meet their basic physical and emotional needs. Reaching out to others and relying on kin communities has allowed our species to survive.

Animals use touch to help regulate through grooming, playing, and lounging on each other. Babies are not left to themselves to self-soothe. They engage with people in their environment to settle their distress. People are meant to carry their emotions with others. But too often, we focus on self-regulation, chastising ourselves when we struggle to manage moments of despair and turmoil.

Sensing Daphne's anger growing as fear and shame underneath expand, I use my professional demeanor to calm her and offer assurance that she is not in this alone. My breath slows. Her breath joins mine. When people are processing instability, the brain operates in a peculiar way—they're on edge, reactive, or snippy. The insecurity of losing ties to culture, safety, and loved ones through death or separation provokes the brain to protect and procure resources.

Some fall into a dazed funk; others try to escape the turmoil through drug abuse or risky behaviors. Daphne bounces between both. At baseline, she buzzes with inspiring creativity and a warm presence. But she hasn't been at baseline since before her arrival in the United States. Yearning for a sense of comfort, she suffers alone, not wanting others to see her pain.

Isolation doesn't mean she's more connected to herself—it's the opposite. As she creates more and more barriers with others, she also strengthens the wall between parts of herself. She finds it difficult to relate to herself, let alone others. Community members, neighbors, even those passing by might be willing and eager to lend their support. But her closed doors keep them out.

Balancing Reinvention with Authenticity

Daphne wants her dark past to stay hidden in the basement. When disturbing memories of being bullied at school or waiting for detention guards to kill her surface, she avoids them in any way she can. I have to clear a path through her shame and humiliation to see where growth can come from. Turns out, it's not from a deep dive into the traumatic events of her past; it's in a space and purpose larger than herself.

Daphne might be physically safe, but she is in an existential crisis: how to balance reinvention with authenticity. Daphne's turmoil has shattered her sense of self. One of the loneliest experiences that I've seen in my patients isn't being alone but feeling severed from oneself. What haunts her are the remnants of her past and the emptiness of a future she won't allow herself to imagine.

Daphne is reckoning with the dissonance between the life she once imagined she'd have and the one she's currently living. This is the crisis of purpose. She's asking not only *What am I here for?* but *Who do I become now, in the wake of what I've lost?*

I help her manage the tug-of-war between the self she's always known and the one she's still discovering. A strong sense of self can be anchored in core values while also open to adaptation and exploration.

Beneath her stories, I catch glimpses of an entrepreneurial instinct to build and leave behind something that matters. She dreams of creating an empire for her family as her legacy. And yet she hesitates, a quiet voice asking if she's too late: *Did I miss my chance?*

Purpose isn't a fixed point on a map or a calling that you discover once and for all; it's an evolving story you write. Purpose is often developed in the wake of rupture. During my sessions with Daphne, we hold the question of *Who do I want to become?* throughout and create space for her to rehearse new versions of herself.

Daphne's sense of purpose is rooted in being a source of strength and support for those she loves, growing into her fullest potential and empowering the next generation to believe in what's possible. Many people see personhood as interwoven with loved ones and future generations, and such is the case for Daphne. Her personal growth isn't just about her; it's about who she is becoming within a larger story. For most people, purpose is embedded in something larger than themselves—wanting to make the world, nature, or the next generation a little better.

For Daphne, creating jewelry is a way to celebrate and share the rich overlooked culture of her homeland with the wider world. Every morning, she writes down her dream of a company, envisions herself selling her jewelry to large stores, and feels the pride that would come with mentoring girls from her home country on entrepreneurship. This ten-minute daily practice scaffolds her energies and time throughout the year. Whenever she falls into a pit of despair, she grabs on to her purpose to help pull herself out.

Psychology and neuroscience both show that people who vividly imagine their future selves are more likely to persist through challenges. And that's not all—the more senses you recruit to imagine your future self, the more likely you are to manifest it into your reality. Neurosurgeon James Doty offered a way to embed purpose and intention into your subconscious: by cultivating a mindful awareness of your goal, writing it down, reading it aloud, and visualizing it daily.

As Daphne engages more in her aspirations and allows herself to dream, she starts to let go of her past. Within six months, she begins making her own jewelry—beadwork that echoes her homeland—and starts asking people for advice on how to sell. Within a year, she has created an online store. While the separation from her family and loss of her connections still loom large, they are now placed adjacent to purpose. She glides from silence to liberation to voice.

Daphne never "finds" herself in the colloquial sense. When she stops treating self-discovery as a destination and embraces it as an ongoing process—one she has more control over—she is able to better define her purpose to help scaffold her goals. The key to knowing oneself isn't locking in an identity—it's staying open to an evolution of who you want to be, which can define your purpose.

Daphne's jewelry had always been more than beads and stone; it was a way to carry her family's story into the world. After a culture blog featured her work, orders exploded. Then came the message: A national distributor offered to triple production and guarantee steady income—she could secure legal backing for her asylum case. But there was a price. She would have to outsource to factories and remove the intricate symbols that gave her work its soul. For them, it was efficiency. For her, it was the same quiet erasure she had once risked her life to escape. Doubting herself, she asks me, "What should I do? How do I decide?"

I am reminded of what a former mentor told me when I was in a career dilemma: "Go to where the best of you can thrive." Daphne has done the work. She has developed a stronger sense of who she is and what matters most in her life, so now she is better equipped to find grace and clarity in her decisions. We map her decision against her purpose—to provide for her family, preserve her culture, and mentor young women—and the answer comes into focus.

She counters with a plan to grow by hiring and training women in her community. The distributor agrees. While the profits are smaller, the gain is in protecting the meaning that fuels her work. Daphne is proud of her ability to allow her dreams to be bigger than her fears.

It turns out that the most authentic people I know aren't those who never change. They're the ones who intentionally evolve, who regularly question their beliefs and are willing to grow even when it's not comfortable. Perhaps the most authentic thing we can do is embrace our capacity for change.

Action Tools for Beyond Goals

A. Who Are You?

1. What's underneath your hustle? Being busy isn't the same thing as being fulfilled. Burnout often comes from achievement without alignment, so while you might be productive, you might not feel grounded. What are some of your past goals and what purpose fueled them?

2. Learn who you are by how you are in relation to others. Identity is shaped in connection. Purpose starts when you notice what enlivens you and how you show up in relationships. When have you felt a deeper connection to someone or something beyond yourself? What roles or identities do you hold that shape who you know yourself to be, and what do they draw out in you? Let your purpose build, one relationship at a time. Create an identity snapshot after important interactions—who were you in that moment?

3. Name the masks and shrink the gap. Everyone wears masks. Purpose begins when you realize where and why you're wearing them. In which situations do you find yourself masking? What do you hide or exaggerate, and what's the personal cost or benefit of doing so? What is the mask protecting? Chronic masking leads to a gap between yourself and others. Try showing more of yourself where you usually hold back and see how that feels.

B. Who Do You Want to Be?

4. Check to see if your values, identities, and behaviors are aligned. Purpose emerges from coherence—when what you do reflects who you are and what you care about. When unsure about how you should act or what you should do, ask yourself, *Where will the best of me thrive?*

5. Develop your purpose through aspiration. When instability freezes who you know yourself to be, rely on who you want to

become. Your future self can guide today's choices. Who do you want to be in five years? Not in terms of titles but in character, values, and impact? Use this vision as a filter for current decisions. If an opportunity, habit, or relationship doesn't bring you closer to that future self, reconsider its place in your life.

8

Corrective Experiences: Ghosts in the Nursery

Every time my kids visit my mother's house—the house where I grew up—they bounce on the inflatable mattresses, gallop in circles around the ficus plants, and fill the living room with the hysterical laughter that comes with a carefree life. The same Asian art scrolls of protective tigers and the three-friends-of-winter motif of bamboo, pine, and plum blossoms cover the walls. But the room doesn't speak to them the same way it does to me.

After my father was kidnapped and assaulted in an attempted murder, I retreated to that living room for what felt like a decade. What my kids know as a place of warmth, I felt as cold and foreboding. For months, I struggled alone as a latchkey kid. I learned how to find comfort in stillness. Comfort with silence.

My ghosts were born in that living room. But my kids might know only the excitement of snow days and a mother who chaperones field trips. They won't see the disorienting terror and guilt that lives in my bones after I saw my father's knife wounds as he lay in a shock trauma unit.

In my childhood mind, crime touched only families who lived in neighborhoods where empty syringes and needles littered the playgrounds. My house had doors and locks; my refrigerator was fully stocked. Who was I to complain of suffering when I never had to worry about winter coats or food on the table? Confused and embarrassed about the violence, I hid its effects from everyone—even myself.

I learned to remove the parts of myself that juggled powerlessness and fear. Instead, they were molded into intuition. A sense of helplessness directed my purpose of serving others who suffered in silence. Many people become physicians to save lives; I wanted to ease suffering. But in the early years of my career, before I had kids, I began questioning my work, drawn by a force that was larger than myself and out of my control.

The ghosts of my past—the undigested, unmetabolized feelings of despair, loneliness, and guilt from my father's experiences—were driving my career choices in another form of repetition compulsion: I couldn't save my father, but perhaps I could help other people around the world who were touched by violence. What I didn't realize was that these ghosts were steering me toward increasingly dangerous situations that left me asking myself, *Why am I doing this work?* and *Is this it for my life?*

Before I had the chance to really engage with these questions about my career, I became pregnant. Previously contained fears and worries suddenly emerged as pregnancy unleashed anxiety about how to protect and care for a newborn whom I knew I would fiercely love.

Mothering crumbled who I knew myself to be. Before, my questioning seemed a useful existential practice, but after I had a child, those questions pummeled me. Days and nights with the newborn blended. I was doubly confused—on the one hand, I was immobilized at the idea of my baby being attached to me like Velcro. On the other, I was heavy with guilt and longing for her in the rare moments when she wasn't in my arms.

Becoming a parent taught me that while I can prepare lunches and playdates, I can't always prepare for broken limbs from falling off the swing or my children's confusion when a close friend suddenly stops talking to them. Just when I'm feeling confident about my ability to manage my kids, they throw a curveball that leaves me unsure of my capacities. After becoming a mother, I had a new purpose: to help my children become resilient, caring, and well-adjusted humans.

I won't block them from experiencing adversity, whether it's not getting the purple plate they want or suddenly having to uproot their lives into two homes. We can't protect our children from all adversity and tragedy, but as a mother, I believe my purpose is to help them manage the instability that is integral to life. My role is to help them gain the skills needed to get through the hard times. What I hadn't realized was that part of my purpose included creating a corrective experience for my past.

Parenting allows me to re-create the sense of guidance and joy that was abruptly cut short in my own childhood. Through parenting, I have the honor of offering my children the playfulness I longed for. Warmth, structure, routine, and doting love are paired with play: carefree afternoons in the park toppling over from cartwheels and handstands, dancing in the kitchen, and singing wildly out of tune.

Clearly, the ghosts of my past chiseled my career choices in developing a purpose to help those suffering in isolation from violence around them. Yet my focus now shifts toward my past's effects on my parenting. I want stability for my kids but fear they won't have the grit and survival skills I gained from my suffering. And then I ask myself: *Do I really want my children to hurt as I did?* No, I don't. And, frankly, suffering will find them, regardless.

We all have ghosts from our past that color the lens through which we engage with the world. It turns out that corrective experiences—positive, meaningful encounters that fill in and repair gaps of the past—are a hidden source of energy that help us move through the afflictions of our lives.

Whether through re-parenting ourselves, learning how to re-love, or taking care of ourselves in a deeply needed way, corrective experiences are an untapped source of strength that you might be engaging in without even realizing it. One's purpose is often a quiet echo of the wounds one carries, a longing to mend what was broken.

The child who felt invisible grows into the adult who craves recognition. The people who were told they were "too much" now seek spaces where their fullness is embraced. Those who knew scarcity become relentless in their pursuit of security. Those who grew up in chaos are drawn to the promise of dependability.

Whether we realize it or not, we spend our lives weaving together the threads of what was missing, stitching together a new narrative in which we are seen, heard, and valued in ways we previously were not. Repairing the past often serves as a compass guiding our choices, our relationships, and our deepest desires.

Understanding purpose as a pursuit of a corrective experience isn't just for therapy patients—it's fundamental to how you navigate the world, shaping the way you interpret challenges, respond to uncertainty, and build relationships. When you recognize that many of your goals stem from a desire to repair past wounds, you gain deeper insight into your motivations and behaviors, allowing you to make more intentional choices about your future. Corrective experiences can serve as a foundation to guide your life's purpose in multiple ways.

First, corrective experiences that fill the emotional void of your past help to process and reframe effects of past hurts on present-day behaviors and perceptions. Once you identify your ghosts and see them for what they are, you can thaw the childhood emotions that were frozen for good reason. As an adult, you are more capable of managing the fear, confusion, and unknowing than you were as a child.

Second, they can stop negative habits from trickling down to the next generation. Plenty of clinical anecdotes and psychological studies have shown that parents' struggles are passed down to the next generation when parents are emotionally unavailable or overly punitive, overly involved or permissive.

Third, corrective experiences can reveal parts of yourself that were long covered. Ghosts of the past have a way of controlling your emotional energy, leaving you with a narrow band of acceptable emotions. Through positive engagements with your children, significant others, work, and life experiences, you find a sense of pride and self-confidence. Examining the effects of adversity on your rela-

tionships long after the instability is over can lead to a deeper healing purpose—not just for you, but for generations to come. It starts
with understanding the influences that shaped who you are today.

Where Are You From?

If you're trying to give someone directions to your home, you need
to know where they're coming from. The same is true for yourself. If
you're trying to navigate to a certain place—a successful career,
healthy parenting, long-term relationships—you need to know
where you're coming from.

Whether we like it or not, we are all influenced by the norms of
our childhoods, no matter how unhealthy or harmful those norms
may have been. Your childhood, hometown, and sense of home are
places that never quite leave you.

There's a Buddhist belief that our lives are merely part of a con-
tinuous stream of life—our existence includes the essence of our
ancestors. Interconnected, we are merely continuing a play that they
started long ago. Part of a larger whole, more than separate individuals, we are never truly alone.

This is true of our actions as well—they are influenced by those
who preceded us. We can take on the responsibility to learn from
their experiences and wisdom to apply to our own lives. This is one
reason why so many Buddhist families focus on honoring elders
and have ceremonies to respect past generations. We need a way to
acknowledge the presence of ancestors within us, both the savvy and
astuteness acquired through their life challenges as well as their
wounds and injuries.

Clinical care and research clearly show that past adversities can
have lasting effects on people long after the threats are gone, despite
their efforts to numb, suppress, or avoid painful memories.

In the mid-twentieth century, scientists uncovered a link between history and biology. They found that trauma doesn't just
shape the mind—it leaves imprints on the body, and the effects are
seen for generations. This concept, called *intergenerational trauma*, is

the passing down of emotional wounds, stress responses, and psy-chological patterns from one generation to the next.

The concept was first described when studies of survivors of the Dutch famine during World War II showed that children born during the food shortage had higher risks of obesity, diabetes, and mental-health disorders decades later—even though they had never experienced the famine themselves. Subsequent studies showed that the effects of trauma could be passed down for generations through family behaviors, cultural narratives, and even biological changes at the genetic level.

Although most of us aren't thinking about how intergenerational traumas are affecting us, we should. They influence how we see ourselves, our worth, and our potential in life. Through my decades of clinical practice, I've come to believe that life is full of wounded people bumping into each other.

◆　◆　◆

Emily enters her first therapy session carrying the weight of exhaustion—an accumulation of a middle-aged person's responsibilities that seem to stretch in every direction. She is a full-time professional, the primary caretaker of teenagers, is managing the signs of menopause, and now she's the primary support for her aging father, who leans on her for nearly everything. The burden is relentless.

She describes her father's latest transgression with a mix of disbelief and fury. That afternoon, her father spent hours gossiping to his friends, painting her as an ungrateful daughter who ignores him at every turn. The injustice of it gnaws at her: Emily's days, which were already packed with obligations, are now consumed by the unpredictable stress of his behavior—minor disagreements escalating to dramatic arguments, relentless demands for reassurance, and accusations that she doesn't really love him when she tries to set a limit.

In the process, Emily's own life has begun to shrink. Her work is suffering. Time with her partner and children has become an afterthought. And yet, no matter how much she gives, her father's neediness only increases. But the relationship with her father isn't the only cause of Emily's suffering.

She's always had an inexplicable need to prove herself, taking responsibility for her friends when she had no reason to do so. With an underlying sense of guilt at her core, she believes that happiness is something to be earned, not just felt.

Session after session, Emily comes in with similar stories—new iterations of the same complaint. Each time, Emily's frustration carries both rage and guilt in equal measure. She wants to be compassionate, but her body betrays her, recoiling at the thought of another demand from her father. Fearing the resentment will calcify and take her down, she sees no way out.

Over the course of a month, I've learned much more about Emily's father than about Emily. The more she speaks, the more it becomes clear that her father's presence occupies far more mental space than she realizes. Her father is like a rip current—deceptively calm waters until, suddenly, an invisible force drags Emily under. There are moments when things seem fine—almost normal—but then, without warning, her father unleashes a remark so cutting, so dismissive, that Emily finds herself flailing in open water, fighting to stay afloat.

Her father blames her for nearly everything, especially when her father makes a mistake; he absolves himself of responsibility and projects his frustrations onto Emily. She has mastered the art of emotional displacement. Emily, despite years of therapy, has found herself ensnared in the same dance, bracing for the next tidal wave.

With resignation creeping into her voice, she admits that she doesn't believe any amount of self-work will undo the dynamic—her suffering will continue until her father is gone.

And yet, something remains unspoken—an unexamined sliver of agency hidden behind the resignation. The question lingers: Is this really all there is, or is there a way for Emily to reclaim herself and escape from the undertow?

Blind Spots

Many people believe themselves to be introspective because they think about themselves in various situations. Yet thinking isn't the same as reflecting. Rumination is like a car stuck in the mud and spinning its wheels—constant motion but no progress. Fixating on resentment or regret and stewing about what's happened keeps you agitated rather than offering insight.

Emily's exhaustion isn't just from caretaking—it's from an internal battle. She has spent her life responding to her father's demands without questioning her own role in the cycle. The truth is, her father isn't the only one maintaining it.

Emily resists this realization. When I point it out, she pivots, filling the silence with more examples of her father's impossible behavior. I get it. Those stuck in instability often claim they want change, yet they remain impervious to awareness. It's easier to feel like a victim than acknowledge the deeper, unresolved forces at play.

For weeks, Emily sits across from me, arms folded, voice crisp with conviction. She recounts her father's latest crises—another frantic call to Emily in the middle of an important meeting, another accusation of neglect, another impossible demand disguised as a plea. Emily carries it all. "He needs me," she says, exhausted yet righteous. "He has no one else."

Emily is doing what so many of us do with friends—replaying the conversation, dissecting every word, seeking confirmation that, yes, this is infuriating. Validation is comforting, even intoxicating. But I am not her friend. I am her therapist, and my role is not just to affirm her frustration but to help her transform it.

I gently challenge her approach: "What if you didn't respond immediately and sat with the subsequent guilt?"

At first, this concept doesn't compute. "Are you kidding? He'd lash out, guilt me, say I don't love him." She exhales sharply, shifting in her seat. "That's just how he is." She continues with the same narrative, now with shame at her own irritation. "Why do I keep acting like this with him?"

A blind spot. Beneath her frustration is something more complex—the fear of separation. Her father's childhood was steeped in chaos: violent fights, nights in motels, years living in a car. Compassionate by nature, Emily is fiercely protective, mindful that she and her father only have each other after her mother died during childbirth. She describes them as always there for each other, yet when pressed for examples, a more complicated picture emerges of a relationship marked by intense highs and crushing lows.

There were screaming matches, emotional withdrawal, and moments when Emily navigated life alone, from homework to getting her first period. Sadness was shut down; loneliness was dismissed; and dissent was met with manipulation and guilt, like the prom dress argument that ended with her father yelling, "Fine, get what you want. I guess I'm just a terrible parent for wanting something nice for you!" Despite the volatility, Emily remained tethered to her father's reactions, as if her value depended on being seen, needed, or approved of. They were each other's emotional lifelines, bound more by enmeshment than autonomy.

As an adult, Emily frames this dynamic as "strong family values," defined as guarding her father's well-being, protecting him from loneliness, and tolerating mistreatment because of past trauma. It's not just love—it's an obligation. Even in absence, her father inhabits her mind and body, each thought sparking the same tension and agony.

Self-sacrifice is disguised as devotion. Without specifically being instructed, she's learned that she owes her father her life and that survival requires sacrifice. Emily's unspoken purpose in life is, unbeknownst to her, helping her father feel loved and less abandoned.

Re-Parenting Ourselves

Catastrophes aren't always a single event. For some, it's death by a thousand cuts—subtle but chronic wounds. Many high-achieving, successful individuals minimize their pasts, convinced they've moved on. But suffering doesn't disappear just because it's buried.

Some people dismiss the past entirely, preferring to focus on the present. Many secretly wonder if they should look back or stay in the now. The answer is: Do both. I've found those who are most resistant to their history are often the ones most shaped by it. Some avoid the past because it's too painful; others minimize it, saying, *I didn't have it that bad—no one hit me.* Trauma isn't about how big it is but how big you had to be to deal with it.

Being unseen, unheard, and emotionally invalidated is a trauma of its own. These wounds don't just fade. They become the unspoken rules that dictate how you love, cope, and act out what you once suffered from.

Emily's usual instinct is to vent, allowing her anger to settle in and her exhaustion to persist. Reflexively, she ruminates, seeks support, then repeats. But as we examine this more closely, she opens herself to trying something new. She lets calls go unanswered, long enough to prove to herself that she is not, in fact, her father's emergency responder. She stops cushioning her boundaries with apologies, learning that a simple no is enough. Most crucially, she resists the lifelong urge to absorb her father's distress as her own.

The more we explore, the clearer it becomes: Emily has been living out a story she didn't even know was written for her. She personally had never suffered poverty or major hardships, but the echoes of her father's trauma shaped her.

An adult carrying the weight of intergenerational trauma often moves through the world with an invisible burden—a blind spot of how much the past is steering the present. They may feel an unrelenting drive to prove themselves, pouring energy into work, relationships, and achievements yet never quite shaking the feeling that they are falling short.

Or perhaps they struggle with intimacy, keeping even those they love at a distance, as if history has taught them that attachment always comes with the risk of pain. They become the fixers, the caretakers, the ones who smooth over conflict—an unconscious effort to bring stability to a world that once felt unpredictable.

Emily was often lost in old, unspoken fears: *What if I'm too much?*

What if I'm not enough? Bracing for disappointment even in moments of joy, she scanned for the next potential rupture—history had taught her that stability is fleeting. The past lingered in her body: tight shoulders, clenched jaw, stomach issues at the first sign of conflict, and her nervous system was always a step away from fight, flight, or freeze. And yet, beneath her coping and survival, she had a quiet yearning to be free.

With intention and compassion toward herself and her father, she has chosen to start taking better care of herself—responding to her father only at specific times of the day, prioritizing conversations that excluded venting about her father, allowing herself joy without justification, and finding her voice again through singing in a local choir.

In caring for herself, she realizes she is also mothering the child she was—a little girl who spent her life trying to earn approval that never came. Every night, she imagines sitting beside that young version of herself, wrapping her in a hug, asking about her day, and reminding her that she is deeply lovable. She's giving herself now what she was denied then.

With time and continued boundaries, Emily feels less like an extension of her father's needs and more like the keeper of her own. By acknowledging her father's pain while claiming her independence, she discovers the possibility of life beyond obligation, where her purpose isn't to hold everything together but to allow herself, finally, to be whole.

The most important driver of Emily's success is how often she is able to resist dysfunctional dynamics, accept that her father will never change, and let go of her fantasy that he might.

Recognizing her blind spots—the way past generations shaped her present—gives Emily clarity. Chaos no longer triggers self-blame or frantic overfunctioning. Instead, she anchors herself in a deeper purpose: to re-parent the child she once was. She speaks to herself with the kindness she long reserved for others, sets limits on what she will accept, and allows herself to dance and paint for the joy of it. In these small but profound acts, she isn't just surviving—she's giving herself the care she always longed for.

This is the power of corrective experiences on our ability to heal, find purpose, and steady ourselves during the inevitable ups and downs of life. Our capacity to supplement the hurts of our pasts and our ancestors' with meaningful and positive responses helps not just ourselves but those around us and those who come after us, so we can be positive presences in others' lives. And that, Emily discovered, is the most radical act of healing: choosing a different path.

Thermostat System of Stress

We often think of emotional upheaval as something experienced in the moment—a reaction to hardship, insurmountable challenges, or personal violations. But what if the danger you feel today isn't just your own? What if it was wired into your biology even before you were born?

Emerging research suggests that the traumas endured by your parents are passed down not just through psychological imprints but through genetic ones. Science is getting a better understanding of the biological mechanisms that explain how hurts from a prior generation can shape how you respond to stress.

When a real threat shows up—say, a bear crashing into your campsite—your body launches an acute stress response: adrenaline surges to sharpen your senses, make your heart pound and muscles tense, while cortisol sustains your energy and focus until the bear is gone. In a healthy system, once the bear lumbers away, cortisol works with other signals to wind down the stress response. With chronic stress, that shutdown never fully comes—cortisol stays high, gradually straining your body and mind over time.

Studies with Vietnam veterans and Holocaust survivors with post-traumatic stress disorder have shown that trauma alters stress hormones in ways that can be passed on to the next generation. The surprising finding? Some people with PTSD don't have chronically high cortisol levels—they have *lower* baseline cortisol and *higher* adrenaline.

Why would that be? Chronic stress and PTSD don't follow the

same pattern. In many people with long-standing PTSD, the body shuts down cortisol too quickly. Levels drop or stay unusually low, while adrenaline keeps surging. The result is a nervous system stuck on high alert, as if the danger never ended.

The plot thickens when we consider the next generation. Research indicates that children of parents with PTSD also tend to have lower cortisol, which makes them more susceptible to stress and, consequently, to developing PTSD themselves—even if they never directly experience trauma.

Think of it as an operating system update that you never signed up for. If a mother's body learns that the world is dangerous and unpredictable, her biology prepares her children to be hyperalert and ready to face threats, real or imagined. In modern society, we have far more psychological stressors than physical ones. There are no woolly mammoths charging after us.

So the inherited vigilance can show up as anxiety, difficulty regulating emotions, or a tendency to shut down under pressure, all because the body is primed for a world that once required constant vigilance. These people may startle easily, overreact to minor stressors, and have difficulty calming down after conflict. Some may struggle with trust, interpret neutral situations as threatening, and have a relentless drive to stay in control because their bodies are wired to expect chaos.

This intergenerational transmission of trauma highlights the dance between nature and nurture. While DNA gives the blueprint, experiences—particularly traumatic ones—can modify how the genes express themselves, a concept known as epigenetics. Genes themselves aren't changed, but traumatic events may affect how DNA is expressed.

It's similar to baking a cake—the ingredients aren't changed, but if the temperature of the oven is raised or lowered, it will change how the cake rises or how dense it is. If a parent has low cortisol due to trauma, the child may inherit a similar stress response. This field has promising explanations as to why trauma impacts the offspring of a trauma survivor, although the research is mostly on animal models.

The good news? Trauma might be inherited, but healing might be too. Emerging research suggests that mindfulness, psychotherapy, social support, and even physical activity can help reverse these epigenetic changes. In other words, what we inherit isn't a life sentence—it's a script. And with awareness, we have the power to rewrite it.

Ghosts in the Nursery

Leo has brought his eight-year-old son to see me for help with behavioral problems. The young boy sits perfectly still, staring at his shoes while his father rattles on: "He is unappreciative, hyperactive, and reckless!" Interspersed with stories about his own childhood and the beating he would have received for such attitudes and behavior, Leo lashes out in anger: "Sit still!" and "Don't talk back to me!" despite the child's neither moving nor talking. Forged in the fire of frustration rather than reflection, the father expresses his own helplessness with anger. "Fix him, Doc," he pleads.

Leo has never thought of himself as unkind. Strict, perhaps. Protective—most definitely. But he considers himself a good father: The world isn't fair and it's his role to toughen up his son so he won't be taken advantage of. When his son cried about being teased at school, Leo said, "Don't be weak." If his son was nervous about joining a new group, Leo sighed and said, "Get over it, you'll be fine." It was the way his father had spoken to him, and hadn't he turned out strong? He learned to survive.

What's strikingly clear is that there is nothing inherently wrong with this child; his father is projecting his own hurts onto his son. Every time I try to speak to the child, Leo cuts in with examples of how hard his life was at the same age.

His stories are locked in his memory in vivid detail—the smell of the leather of the belt that lashed him, the brand of cigarette that burned his arm, the feel of the velvet couch onto which he was thrown. Clinicians have a term for this: *screen memories*, a fixation on specific details that allow people to survive by burying emotion.

This is the luxury of panic—when under threat, you can bury emotions. But after the threat, the buried emotions reemerge, despite your best efforts. They permeate relationships and become the "ghosts" in children's nurseries.

Psychoanalyst Selma Fraiberg coined the term *ghosts in the nursery*, to describe the unfathomed adversities of the past that create struggles in relationships that leave people drained and confused. She wrote, "In every nursery there are ghosts. They are the visitors from the unremembered past of the parents and the uninvited guests at the christening." These ghosts can appear in all aspects of parenting, even in infancy, from feeding and sleep rituals to toilet training and discipline.

"A Mother Can Only Hear Her Child's Cries if Her Own Cries Are Heard"

Through our sessions, I recall the words of Selma Fraiberg, "A mother can only hear her child's cries if her own cries are heard." The only shot I've got to help this child is to help Leo feel heard and seen. So instead of working directly with the child, I first work with Leo to gently reveal the ghosts that perpetuate his own suffering and create suffering in his child.

"He's so ungrateful!" Leo explodes, wanting me to see how difficult his child is making his life. "He left an entire bowl of cereal in the sink—what a waste! Who does he think he is, throwing away good food that I'm working to pay for!" Clearly, Leo was treated similarly and never had permission to express his childhood sadness and helplessness.

Before inviting Leo to empathize with his child, I spend multiple sessions listening to the various ways in which adults in his life caused him harm. After each story, I pause to slow him down and validate how scary and sad that must have been. Repeatedly, I give compassion and concern for his childhood self, and soon, Leo is able to as well.

Leo becomes incrementally more able to reflect on his parenting behaviors. When he catches himself acting in a similar manner as someone who hurt him in the past, we engage in reappraisal—finding a way to tell the story of his painful past that honors the suffering and hardship but also acknowledges his resilience and how he learned to adapt.

He notes a time last week when he and his son argued over his son's music being too loud. Leo opened his mouth to tell him what an ungrateful and disrespectful child he was and that he needed to show respect. But before he could speak, he saw it. The way his son flinched—not from a physical attack, but it was clear: Here was a son who didn't respect his father. Suddenly, Leo wasn't looking at his son anymore. He was looking at himself as a boy, aching for a comfort that never came.

"My dad grew up in a different time. He was dirt-poor—like, living in filth. Every time he talked down to me, though, it made me want to prove to him and everyone else that I would be something. I would get out of that hellhole. And I did. I worked my ass off and even went to trade school. I decided I would make something of myself in a way he never did," he says as pride starts to emerge.

Just as ghosts hiding in the nursery can perpetuate instability and chaos in the family, bearing witness to them can reactively spark one's purpose: "I'll never be like my father!" or, as Leo said, "I'll make something of myself." While he is giving more to his child than he himself had growing up, until now, he hasn't been able to see the ghosts that were directing his relationships, experiences, and perceptions of reality. He believed that preparing his son for the world meant making him tough. But what if real strength isn't about hardening but softening?

While Leo was clear that he had been mistreated as a child and was therefore able to identify his ghosts, many people are not. Studies have shown that the majority of adults have had some form of adverse childhood experience, so we are all walking around with invisible ghosts influencing us.

Parents believe they are present and attentive—look at their research on sippy cups and sleep schedules. But perhaps they are attentive to the wrong thing. Classic evidence shows that the best predictor of secure attachment is the parents' ability to understand their own early life experiences and how the past plays a role in the present.

Parents are just the vessels through which their children arrive. Whether they are luxury yachts or motorboats, junks or dinghies, people have their own constitutional makeup and experiences that guide the rudders, steer children away from large rocks, and warn them of upcoming dense fog and thunderstorms. Parents need to understand what their cornerstones are in order to guide them appropriately. When adults think about having children, most of them consider their own childhood experiences. Perhaps they make resolutions that they won't be as harsh as their fathers or as invalidating as their mothers. Even if the parents are from stable, loving homes, they will not always respond perfectly to a child's tears and hurts.

Parenting never ends; they always worry about their children, deep into their later years if they are so lucky. One's children having children becomes a bulwark against aging, making parents into grandparents and giving them purpose and new life. Parents push through discomfort to hope for something better. But often, hurts from the past, like ghosts, surface in parents' daily lives. When trauma goes unresolved, it unconsciously shapes a person's identity, behaviors, and beliefs, making it difficult to break free from the patterns of prior generations.

But herein lies the gift of parenting: Many parents who had childhoods deprived of security, care, and connection can undergo a corrective experience when they raise their children and learn how to re-parent themselves.

Angels in the Nursery

Raising children may be a clear purpose for parents, as it opens the world to something much larger than the individual self. While they may recoil and want to reclaim their freedom and independence at times, most are also deeply grateful for the opportunity to shape their children's future, giving them a grounded sense of meaning and purpose.

Yet there are also hidden motives that influence behaviors. We all seek out corrective experiences in work, love, and life that we may not be aware of. Perhaps it's a nurturing friendship with an older person that allows you to have a corrective experience to work out your family dramas; a supervisor who sees the potential no one else ever has; or a loving partner with whom you can work through what you needed in the past. The desire to fulfill what one didn't get in the past can often fuel a person's life purpose.

For many people, purpose isn't just about chasing a passion—it's about healing a past wound. Studies show that some of the most generous, compassionate, and supportive people are those who have seen hard knocks in childhood. When we are challenged, we can let it harden us or we can use it to fuel a deeper sense of meaning. Many people unconsciously turn their greatest struggles into their life's work, not to erase the past, but to rewrite its impact.

After I spend many months seeing only Leo, I ask to meet with his child alone. As soon as the door closes behind Leo, tension shifts in the room. I expect resistance, maybe guarded silence. But although this child has been raised in the shadow of his father's harshness, his tenderness is startling. He speaks about a ladybug he saw at recess and his joy at finding painted rocks on his walk back from school. It's as if he has built a secret cave inside himself where gentleness can still exist.

I ask the child who his favorite people are, which I sometimes include in a *social mapping* exercise: drawing concentric circles around the child in the center and asking him to place people within each circle based on how close he feels to them.

Huddling next to him in his small little circle is Mr. Tucker, his physical education teacher. Unlike his father, Mr. Tucker met his curiosity with patience. Volatility at home was met with Mr. Tucker's steady and predictable presence at school. He's had this same teacher since kindergarten. On the days when the child came to school appearing tense after his father's sharp words, Mr. Tucker noticed. He never pried or pushed, just gave him a basketball and said, "Let's see that shot," or asked him to set up the cones or help with an obstacle course. Over time, the small gestures became something bigger.

Mr. Tucker unknowingly offered the child an unspoken truth: Support doesn't have to come from home—it can be built through people who choose to show up.

A single steady presence won't erase the wounds of an unpredictable environment, but it can offer children something just as powerful: the belief that they are lovable, worthy, and important. Plenty of research on protective factors in child development shows that a supportive adult can serve as a buffer against the negative effects of adversity. That, to me, seems a worthy purpose: to become the *angel* in the nursery for those around us.

Action Tools for Corrective Experiences

A. Manage the Ghosts in Your Nursery

1. Map your emotional inheritance. Unseen narratives and past experiences often steer present decisions. Family patterns tend to echo across generations, so the past is embedded in how you love, lead, and live. Write down three emotional habits you learned from your caretakers (e.g., conflict avoidance, perfectionism, emotional shutdown). Ask a trusted person in your family about experiences (e.g., war, immigration, abuse, poverty) that shaped your generational ghosts.

2. Notice the drive for corrective experiences. Unmet childhood needs tend to show up as adult longings for love, validation, and security. Without awareness, you may organize your life around a desire to correct the past. Write about the situations where you overreact—what unmet need might be speaking? What resentment or regrets are you fixated on? Is there a separate and distinct internal battle playing a role? Identify one way you're seeking validation externally (e.g., through achievement or by being overly friendly) and try offering it to yourself internally.

B. Repair What You Didn't Get in the Past

3. Shine a light on your blind spots. Blind spots are the ghosts of your past that crave a corrective experience. The past shows up in the places that matter most, typically relationships and work. What are the ghosts of your past and how do they show up in different parts of your life? For example, in relationships or teams, is there a problematic default to caretaker, hero, scapegoat, or peacemaker? Where does the desire to repair what you didn't receive in the past play a role?

4. Highlight the angels in your nursery. Even if you're living under extremely difficult circumstances, one safe relationship can change your story. Who is someone, past or present, who

made you feel safe, seen, or believed in? Write about them. If no one comes to mind, become that angel for your younger self. Imagine the child you once were and offer the warmth, attention, and love you needed. Think about your current life—where can you serve as this safe figure for someone else?

9

Mattering

Before having kids, I thought I knew what purpose looked like. Working at the individual and system level with children and families facing human rights violations and forced displacement was my north star.

People who knew me were well aware that I wanted kids and often asked what would happen then: How would I balance humanitarian work with motherhood? I barely understood the question. Why should anything change? I figured I'd just carry them on my back through disaster zones—mothers have been doing that in every corner of the world for centuries.

Then I became a mother, and my identity collapsed in on itself. The world I had built, one of movement, war zones, makeshift homes in foreign countries, became uninhabitable. Malaria pills and checkpoints, once mere inconveniences, suddenly seemed reckless instead of noble. The call to serve others, once so clear, was drowned out by something stronger: the primal urge to protect my own. When I was pregnant, I replaced interviews with former child soldiers with baby journals, tracking the size of my growing baby in an album: a rice kernel, a pea, then a peach.

My life was divided into two phases: before children and after. *Before* children, I moved through the world untethered. *After*, every decision felt like a thread pulling me back to them. Now, almost a decade later, my two kids are old enough to clear their dinner plates, brush their own teeth, and navigate schoolyard conflicts. And for the first time, they went off on a summer trip without me. I had no one to feed. No one to tuck in. This should have felt like freedom. Instead, it felt like an unraveling.

So when my Ethiopian friend asked me to work in Tigray—still marked by the devastation of war crimes and crimes against humanity—I said yes. In my work, I only take on initiatives with local partners who understand the community context and priorities. In this case, the leadership and vision are already there; my task is to strengthen the capacity behind them. The most meaningful part of my work has always been collaborating with people who are shaping their own communities. *Maybe this will bring me back to life,* I thought.

Yet instead of feeling purposeful, I felt porous. Unmoored.

I still had a purpose, and arguably, helping children who experienced war crimes is at the top of the list of meaningful ways to spend one's time. But my purpose quickly faded, as I lacked what psychologists call *existential mattering*—that is, when people feel their lives are of value and significance to the world at large. At that moment, I didn't really think that what I was doing in Ethiopia mattered that much.

I moved through the *woredas* as a shadow of myself, making mistake after mistake: I packed a mosquito net I didn't need but forgot hand sanitizer. I ate injera with my left hand—an insult in Orthodox Christian culture. I miscalculated schedules and forgot extra gifts. Of course, none of that mattered as much as the stories I heard.

For two years, this region was starved of attention, its people violated not just by war but by silence. Villages were razed. Women were violated in ways meant to break the generations that came after them. Children were forced to watch their parents murdered. Now, the ones who survived are left with nothing, as droughts, floods, and famine ensue. Children had been out of school for three years, too hungry to study, too devastated to care. No longer dreaming of a future, they wondered, *Is this just how life is?*

One evening, I forced myself out of my room to meet someone deeply involved in the region's recovery efforts. Friends insisted we should connect, given our shared concerns, as he was at the center of rebuilding a collapsed system against impossible odds. As we spoke, I found myself leaning in, drawn to his unwavering resolve. His words carried the weight of someone who had seen too much but refused to turn away.

We spoke about philosophy, the human spirit, and what the community had endured. Then he said, "I want people to come to Tigray to learn what it means to be human."

I don't speak for Tigray, nor do I claim expertise in its politics. What I witnessed—in the community and in a friend—wasn't beauty born of suffering but of people insisting each other mattered: bringing food, checking on neighbors, walking friends home after dark. What moved me was their constancy in showing up.

This man had the ability to leave the country—I would have understood if he did, as he had to be exhausted from taking care of the region and he had a young family who'd lived through the bloodshed; how could he sleep at night? I asked him, and without hesitation, he said, "I sleep well at night. More work needs to be done here; this is my home."

This was the true power of mattering. When we have a purpose that involves a cause larger than ourselves, we can sleep at night—even when bombs fall in the distance. Purpose isn't about individual success. It's about choosing—again and again—to matter to someone else.

While I think it's important for my kids to see that I'm part of something larger, it's also important for me to remember that purpose isn't static; it evolves and adapts with time and experiences. Embracing the changes in one's sense of purpose can lead to growth.

In Tigray, I saw it clearly: The community here had endured unthinkable loss, yet they held each other up. They grieved together, rebuilt together, and reminded one another—through shared meals, quiet gestures, and relentless care—that no one was meant to bear life alone.

When I got back home, life continued in its familiar rhythm. My children returned, routines resumed, and the ache of the experience of being physically apart from them settled into memory. But now I knew that mattering wasn't just about being needed—it was about anchoring ourselves to something beyond our own existence. When we do, we learn to navigate the uncertainties, the losses, and the moments of doubt. Not by resisting them, but by grounding ourselves in the connections that hold us steady.

Purpose isn't something you stumble upon in a single moment of clarity, nor is it a destination to reach and claim. Instead, it's an intricate web of relationships and actions that pull you through life's inevitable turbulence. And the science behind it is clear: The more deeply connected you are to something larger than yourself—whether it's a cause, a community, or a sense of shared humanity—the more resilient you become in the face of hardship.

Purpose doesn't reside in *what* you do; it lies in *why* you do it. And that *why* is shaped by the relationships you nurture and the lives you touch. When we feel connected, know we matter, and have a clear purpose, we're better equipped to weather life's ups and downs.

That's not just a comforting idea; it's what your body is built to do. Researchers have found that when people feel that they matter—when they know they are contributing to something greater than themselves—their bodies respond. When you are going through times of stress, a commitment to others steadies your heart rate, strengthens your immune system, and spikes your mental resilience.

Serving as a psychological and physiological anchor, purpose gives us something to hold on to when everything around us feels like it might unravel. It's our motivation—a compass to guide our actions.

But we need to know that our actions actually matter. While most people don't live in active war zones, we all have access to developing our sense of mattering in the work we do, the communities we're embedded in, and the relationships we're influenced by.

Over the years, I've asked people from every corner of my work—

from individuals in private practice, communities in humanitarian contexts, and executives in corporations—what gives their life meaning. At first, people talked about their goals: raising children, building careers, creating something new. But as our conversations deepened, another truth surfaced—the need to feel that they actually mattered. Purpose is about having direction. Mattering is about knowing that direction will lead to somewhere worth going.

People who have both aren't just chasing milestones but are driven by the belief that their presence and efforts make a difference. Those who lack one or the other often feel stuck, either working hard toward goals no one seems to value, or believing they are important but unsure how to channel it. When purpose and mattering come together, something shifts: Achievements feel more rewarding. Setbacks feel more survivable. And life becomes less about making it to the end and more about making it count.

So we don't need to focus so much on standing out. It's more about standing with. Mattering to others isn't found in grand gestures or perfect decisions but woven into the small daily acts of showing up for the belief that even in suffering, there is connection. Instead of a single destination, mattering to others is a practice, a commitment to stepping outside of ourselves and into the lives of others.

Mattering Magnets

Chalky white dust lingered in the air, making it difficult to see. Fourteen-year-old Esperance cautiously and aimlessly held her arms out in front of her and shuffled her feet among broken concrete fragments. Her home had collapsed; the roof slanted at a forty-five-degree angle off the left side, wanting to touch the ground.

It was January 12, 2010, and a 7.0 M_w earthquake had demolished the public infrastructure, iconic buildings, and so much else in Haiti. An estimated 222,570 people died, though some reported an additional hundred thousand victims, as 90 percent of the buildings in Léogâne were destroyed. Within thirty seconds, the earthquake devastated the country at previously unimaginable levels, reducing homes and offices to rubble and separating families forever.

One of those families was Esperance's. After finishing her homework at her friend's place after school, she walked toward home for dinner. Suddenly, the ground began trembling beneath her, catapulting her into a run toward her home—one that she now had difficulty finding.

Having been shaken from side to side, her house was now an unrecognizable pile of broken rubble. After walking around in shock, looking for her parents and sister, she stood perfectly still as her mind spun furiously. *Where's my family? What am I supposed to do? Where should I go?* Within two hours, the country was shaken by eight aftershocks with magnitudes between 4.3 and 5.9 M_w.

Esperance went to a makeshift shelter in a tent city and tried to sleep during the day so she could stay up walking around at night. Hope dwindling, and with nothing else occupying her time, she watched what was happening around her as if it were on a screen. Throughout the days, she saw *tap-tap* mini-buses jammed with excavators and mothers walking alongside holding toddlers' hands. Sellers squatted next to crooked wooden frames, women in sarongs walked by with a look of mistrust, and young men listlessly leaned against trees.

On top of the devastation from the earthquake was another disaster: sexual predation after social destruction. She had grown accustomed to the yells of girls and women from two years old to seventy-two as they were sexually assaulted when the sun went down. With only a sheet or tarp thrown across a tree limb or stick, there was little protection. Demolished police stations, jails, and prisons left the country in relative anarchy.

Early one night, as Esperance aimlessly wandered around hoping to see a familiar face, she caught a glimpse of someone with a kind eye—a grandfatherly looking man smiled at her. "You seem tired, girl," he said, words wrapping around her like a security blanket. The grandfather spent time talking with her and listening to her story of how she lost her family, and he encouraged her to come to his house for dinner: His wife was cooking and the girl must need a safe place to rest, he said.

Weeping in relief, she joined him. After walking for half an hour, they arrived at a small broken house. A grandmotherly woman greeted her at the door. Behind her were three adult men who quickly took Esperance in, then proceeded to sexually assault her.

One month after the earthquake, the smell of dead bodies trapped under the rubble still permeates the air, and food, water, and security barely exist. With all her guardians and loved ones still unaccounted for and a severe back injury from falling in the rubble that was worsened by the sexual assault, Esperance is meeting with me for a psychiatric affidavit to support her case for humanitarian parole in the United States.

This is the first time I've slept in a tent—not as in camping, but a tent pitched on concrete next to a collapsed office. Many Haitians sleep outside under a tarp or makeshift tent, scared about another aftershock, so I've joined them. When I unzip my tent flap at six A.M., there is already a long line of about twenty to thirty women, children, and men who have been waiting there all night.

Esperance is polite. She moves slowly and sits firmly upright, revealing her exhausted and activated nervous system. She tells me that after she escaped her assailants, she stumbled upon a group of street kids near a tent camp. They clung to her day and night, feeling a sense of togetherness.

"They were always around me, and I ended up liking them. But we had nothing to do all day, so I started to teach." Teaching everything from basic math to telling any stories she could remember, Esperance began to feel stronger. "It was pretty clear they needed me." Esperance feels valued. She means something to these kids and is obviously making a positive difference in their lives.

Her purpose becomes magnetic as she encourages children of all ages to press on and find hope. Replacing helplessness is a spark of motivation—a drive to become a teacher, to inspire, guide, and encourage children to believe in themselves.

Studies show that people are drawn to those who display a sense of purpose and are engaged in what they're doing—and that they have broader and deeper social networks. For better or worse, people want to be close to those who offer a glimpse of opportunity.

This is true for Esperance. While she might not be the loudest or wisest of the group, she is swift in tuning in to the needs of each child. Bearing responsibility for orphaned children reaffirms her purpose in the world and helps keep her afloat through the uncertainties of her day-to-day life.

This new perspective shaped how she perceived herself in this world—now a world in which she matters. Emboldened with a sense of worth, she channels her energy toward encouraging these children.

Feeling more confident about her ability to move through the day, she opens herself to friendship and connection. She affirms her commitment to fulfill their needs for attachment and taps into a sense of pride she hasn't felt in a very long time. Believing that she matters to others and can add to the world gives her the scaffolding she needs to motivate her life.

Paradox of Connection

While most of us will not endure the pain of suddenly losing our loved ones in a natural disaster, we can all learn from those who have. Some people might believe they have nothing in common with those who have suffered most until they bear witness to it and realize our universal human experiences.

Mattering makes a difference in the lives of others, but it also has a profound effect on the individual. Similar to belonging or self-esteem, mattering may be a fundamental human need. One's sense of meaning is built on the foundation of being needed. Those who feel that they are valued and that they have an impact on others—whether it's family, friends, colleagues, or strangers—are more likely to report high levels of well-being. They have greater emotional stability, fewer symptoms of depression, and higher levels of life satisfaction.

It's a virtuous cycle: When you matter, you thrive; when you thrive, you can give more of yourself.

One of the most compelling pieces of evidence for the power of connection comes from one of the longest-running and most robust studies in the history of social science. Psychiatrists George Vaillant and Robert Waldinger tracked the lives of over seven hundred men for more than seventy-five years in what is now known as the Harvard Study of Adult Development.

Following this cohort of men from adolescence into their eighties and nineties, Drs. Vaillant and Waldinger gathered data on everything from their physical health to their social relationships to determine what makes a good life and what factors contribute to healthy aging and well-being. Their cohort went through the normal tribulations that life holds: alcoholism, medical scares, unexpected loss, divorce, and layoffs.

Their findings were clear. Those who had close, warm relationships were happier, healthier, and lived longer than those who didn't. In fact, the quality of their relationships was a better predictor of health and longevity than cholesterol levels, blood pressure, or even genetic predispositions.

It turns out that the key to a long, healthy, and meaningful life is not wealth, fame, or success. It's the quality of our relationships. When we invest in meaningful relationships—when we feel seen, heard, and valued by those around us—we don't just thrive emotionally; we thrive physically as well. Or, as Dr. Vaillant, who was my former supervisor, once told me, "The key to healthy aging is relationships, relationships, relationships."

Despite our busy lives, at the end of the day, we are all humans who have evolved for social connection. In the Stone Age, people had to move beyond the natural world, learn whom to trust, and build alliances to prosper in their clan. From thousands of years ago, when our ancestors survived by creating social ties and engaging in negotiations like bartering food with people they didn't know, to today, when preschoolers barter dolls and trucks, neighbors trade favors, and leaders across sectors strike deals, humans are programmed for connection—even if transactional. Sharing food with the right person meant the favor would be returned at some point.

The sense of connection is based on more than pure transactions, though. Even before we know how to speak, the sense of self is deeply entwined with another. When our caveperson ancestors were suddenly threatened by territorial cave bears or hyenas, their bodies activated a response cascade of hormones and neurotransmitters to speed up heart rates and shunt blood to muscles or brains to get them out of danger.

We might not be running from tigers anymore, but our brains are still wired to respond to threats. Today, the dangers are deadlines and difficult conversations, and one of our best tools for handling them is each other. Your brain has cells that act a bit like mirrors: they fire not only when you do something, but also when you watch someone else do it. Scientists call them *mirror-neurons,* and while their exact role in humans is still being studied, they seem to be part of a broader network that helps us understand actions, read emotions, and connect socially.

When we connect, our mirror neurons light up, letting us feel and respond to each other's emotions as if they were our own—someone else's smile can lift your mood, or their stress can tug at your heart. Those moments of connection can be a powerful buffer against life's pressures.

If your forever-after relationship ends and your best friend comes over to watch movies and order takeout with you, you feel comforted, and your best friend feels the benefit of supporting a loved one. It turns out that caring has bidirectional benefits, and we are longing for these bonds.

Around the world, people are carrying the weight of a fragmented society that no longer connects them in a meaningful way. The rates of social isolation and loneliness and the precursors of depression, anxiety, and suicide have all increased as the solitary person falls through society's cracks.

Caught in a tangle of structural isolation where workers are abandoned by their employers and neighbors are devoid of a shared purpose, people are left with the feeling of being replaceable and undeserving of life. Loneliness is worsened by the burden of being left to navigate life's instabilities alone. The problem is in both loneliness and having to manage the loneliness on one's own.

This is the paradox of connection: Everyone craves more, but few know how to create it. Instead of reaching out to people, we scroll through feeds. In-person conversations are replaced with emojis. Real connection takes intention, vulnerability, and the courage to show up in ways that go beyond a like or a text. Too often, people's idea of connection ends with talking. They assume they're building a bond when they're really just talking about themselves, filling the air with words and transforming the listener into a wall. Connection isn't measured by how much we speak; it's measured by how much we genuinely make room for someone else. No wonder we still feel alone—we haven't been taught how to meaningfully connect to others.

Birds of a Feather Flock Together

If there's something destabilizing, we don't want to see it. We'd rather immerse ourselves in worlds where we're comfortable, where we succeed, and where there are people we trust and cooperate with. While we'd like to believe that opposites attract, research shows that the psychological default is for people to select others who are similar to them from the outset of the interaction.

When we're managing uncertainty, our brains operate in a very different way than when we're not: We're more brittle and quicker to react. We become much more focused on our in-group as it becomes harder to empathize with others. Joining with friends and communities gives a feeling of belonging that creates a sense of inner security so we aren't feeling alone in the instability.

While it may feel safer to gather with those who look like you or who went to the same school as you, true connection is more intimate than that. Just because families and communities are at the center of most societies doesn't necessarily mean there is meaningful connection. Proximity doesn't equal intimacy. Bringing people together matters, but it isn't enough.

You may be surrounded by people at work, at a religious gathering, or at a coffee shop and yet feel completely alone. The opposite is also true—there are times when you're with just one or two companions and you feel all the love in the world.

Feeling a sense of belonging is about more than merely putting a group of people together—just ask anyone who's gone to a cocktail party solo. Guests need some structure and prompting for connection. One can be surrounded by transactional relationships but still feel alone, devoid of any sustained, deep relational bond.

Those who are able to surface through the hard times don't necessarily have the most friends or the most people with a similar demographic or experience around them. When people accept the hardships they can't avoid, they find a purpose that grounds them to who they are and strengthens their ties to others, creating connection, meaning, and impact.

Like-minded friends can help us when we need support and comfort. When I can sense someone minimizing their dream out of fear of society's negative response, I often ask, "What would you do if everyone fully supported you in your decision?" Full support can feel like freedom.

Yet even the safest circles can become places to hide from the stretch of real growth. The stability that we find in comforting friendships may not always challenge us. Being part of the wider, more diverse world can expose us to new ideas that correct us when we're off base. But our inherent nature to seek out like-minded folks comes with the drawback of less exposure to diverse ideas and beliefs. So we're left with a conundrum—we stick with those we know, even if the comfort stunts our growth.

Social Fitness

Self-improvement and anti-aging industries prioritize physical health with strength training, cardiovascular activities, and flexibility exercises. But people rarely train for the kind of fitness that matters just as much: social fitness.

Just as muscles atrophy without use, the ability to connect, listen, and support others erodes without practice. For most people, the problem isn't that they don't want to be there for those they love; it's that they don't know how.

If someone is grieving, struggling, or facing an impossible loss, we hesitate: *What if I say the wrong thing?* We may be scared that instability is contagious, like the flu, and we don't have time for that to happen. Turmoil brings us closer to the edge and we don't want to go there.

Studies show that meaningful relationships aren't built only on big gestures but on repeated, small moments of connection—checking in, listening without trying to fix the problem, sharing in discomfort. Social fitness, like physical endurance, improves with effort. In order to truly matter to the people we love, we have to train ourselves to do the hard work of being present, even when we're unsure how.

Clarifying your inner narratives is an important first step in understanding how you may distance yourself from a loved one who's going through a hard time or just isolate yourself, burrowing in the comfort of nonattachment to another's judgment, perspective, or responsibility. For many, relationships—especially romantic ones—are a constant mirror to one's self-worth. People then pour their energy into the romantic relationship, placing it at the top of the hierarchy of connections, thereby devaluing friendships or family relationships.

As we glide into roles and responsibilities, our connections can become more utilitarian. If we become parents, we say we'll start developing more meaningful connections in a decade or so, especially if we're under the demands of young children and intense careers.

But feeling connected is as important as diet and exercise. If you don't pay attention to your relational health throughout life, you can inadvertently cause damage down the line.

Plenty of research shows that one of the best predictors of a person's well-being is having a social blanket of friends, colleagues, neighbors, and family. People to argue with, talk with, hang out with, trust, get solid advice and help from, all of which you can reciprocate. Although we may believe our lives are overtaken with responsibilities and commitments or punctuated with illness and injuries that slow us down, those are the exact times when we can look to where we matter for guidance.

Even when we are successful in connecting to our self-respect and needs, we are dynamic humans with changing ambitions and priorities, especially in a process of personal growth. There can be a harsh cost when personal growth challenges our connections.

Sometimes we may distance ourselves out of a fear of rejection. *What if they think I'm not doing enough? What if I make things worse? What if I seem insensitive?*

The anticipation of rejection and fear of loneliness whisper to inform us how to make friends, engage in groups, act in public, and even how to think. When we feel a primal jolt of being unwanted, our minds tend to jump to conclusions that may be harmful to ourselves and others, creating unnecessary pain. Our fear of rejection keeps us feeling safe and protected, but it can also harm us.

Feeling unwanted hurts. You might try to avoid conflict in order to avoid criticism. If you're constantly looking for signs you're about to be rejected, you may misinterpret and overreact to what others do, often lashing out with hurt and anger. If this is you, you're not alone.

Many people aren't fully aware of their backstories. They may have a narrative such as "I've always been the outsider in the family" or "I've always been a burden," but rarely is it a full picture. Backstories are rampant with connections made and lost along the way that shaped how people receive love. If you're estranged from your own backstory, you might withdraw at the scent of intimacy, of being known, and of deeply knowing another. Going through relationship after relationship without any real connection is a sign of disconnect with your own backstory.

Many people who come through my office reflect that in general, they feel there's no safe person to talk to. Maybe they'll be negatively judged, stereotyped, or invalidated. So they keep quiet in their struggle alone or engage in thoughts about how they could improve themselves without actually wanting to know. Being curious about your backstory is a necessary foundation to social fitness.

Competition with others and inner obsession with your own self-improvement can slowly whittle away your connections not just to friends, coworkers, and family but also to those you have micro-relationships with: the store clerk, the medical assistant, the neighbors walking their dog. Absorbed in your own ideas, dreams, and conflicts, you might spend more time thinking about the world than actually living in it.

Avoiding our own backstory or pain can keep us from truly showing up for others. But when suffering arrives, we can't hide from it forever. The choice becomes whether to withdraw behind fear, or to bear witness to our own pain in a way that lets us stay connected to those we love.

On Witnessing

Derek spent his life mastering the art of control. His career was built on precision, and he prided himself on his ability to anticipate risks before they materialized. But cancer didn't negotiate, and there was no warning, no courteous waiting for the right moment or a slow reveal. Derek's scans were definitive, the prognosis unforgiving.

"How can I tell my son I'm going to die?" Derek looks at his scuffed leather shoes, his voice quiet in case his twelve-year-old son outside my office door can hear him. "Most days I can't even look at him. I just can't imagine not seeing him start college, get married, or have kids." Recently diagnosed with stage three colon cancer, the fifty-one-year-old father is so crushed by the thought of leaving his son that he has to pull away from him. Worried about their son's sudden disinterest in school, friends, and theater, Derek's spouse has suggested he see me for help.

"I can't even talk to my partner about this. I don't think they can bear to think about it." Derek distances himself from his son to protect him from his own unbearable heartache. Unwilling to allow his loved ones the opportunity to be present with him in his suffering, Derek blocks any meaningful interaction, not realizing that connection to him is precisely what they need. He doesn't recognize that his emotional detachment from his family terrifies them more than the threat of his death.

Derek is now in a parental moral quandary: Does he open up to his son about his fears of death, pain, and the loss of dignity when doing so may cause harm to his son—something that all parents strive to avoid? Unable to share his intimate thoughts and feelings, he withdraws from his most cherished people. He assumes that sharing will cause them to withdraw from him. Terrified of his own fear of dying, he treats himself as if he's contagious. Since he can't bear witness to his own suffering, he can't imagine having others do it.

Kaethe Weingarten, psychologist and founder of the Witness to Witness program, relates the risks of witnessing: There's a risk to holding on to and sitting with loved ones who are suffering. Being in the presence of someone who is deep in the pits of suffering can make us feel extremely incompetent. *Am I saying the right thing? Conveying that I really care?*

Responding is especially hard when the suffering is unexpected. You meet an old friend for coffee and it turns out the week before, his brother was in a tragic car accident. A work meeting turns into an armchair therapy session when your colleague reports the discovery of her spouse's infidelity. You become an inadvertent—and sometimes unwilling—witness to their despair.

How you respond to other people's situations can teach you something about how you respond to your own. Do you shift in your seat with discomfort, grip a coffee cup, or hope you'll get called away immediately? Maybe you actually excuse yourself from the meeting to use the bathroom but never return. Your response to bearing witness to another's suffering may be the first act in understanding how you engage with your own.

Derek moves between two parallel struggles: He's facing his own death and deciding when—and how—to tell his son. The first is an existential and visceral unraveling of his world. Shocked and indignant, he is forced to contend with the fact that this is a problem he cannot fix. He has less than one year to live.

The second struggle is even more daunting for him. "How do I look into his eyes—into the eyes of my little guy who sees me as invincible—and tell him that very soon, I won't be here for him anymore?" As if he has just taken the life of a beloved, he looks down in shame.

Derek believes his son cannot possibly bear his father's suffering and fear. But children often find strength in difficult moments, especially when they don't have to face them alone. When children are made aware of the reality of the situation and another's internal world, it gives them the chance to find empowerment in their own developmentally appropriate way.

Some children might initially protest in defiance, talking back to teachers or bullying peers. Others might turn to humor, trying to make as many people laugh as possible. And then there are those who might find quiet and peace, wanting a routine and schedule to help move them through the day.

Even while suffering, parents can join with their children to contain the chaos of despair—together. But first, it's often a good idea to understand the impact of the situation on themselves so they have a better handle on what they want to relay to the kids and strategize how they'll manage their feelings—even if everything doesn't go as planned. People tend to process their experiences with others, and they should—with a therapist, a loved one, or a friend. But not with their children.

During our work together, Derek first gives words to his terror. He rehearses different versions of how to deliver the reality. Some are more clinical and factual; others are softer, wrapped in metaphors about stars that shine long after they burn out. But each time, his chest stiffens as he imagines his son's face crumpling in confusion; tears glazing his eyes.

Psychologists call this *anticipatory grief*—the mourning that happens before the loss itself. But Derek feels something else too. A consuming sense that he's about to steal his son's childhood, burden him with a weight that can never be fully lifted. Rationally, he knows that shielding him from the truth isn't protective. He's avoiding it.

Yet children are emotional sponges who have a strikingly astute sense of what is left unsaid. It's hard to help children give words and understanding to their fears and worries with parents who are pretending as if there's nothing going on. Silence only forces children to be alone with their thoughts and it has a way of spreading into something often worse than the truth.

Derek thinks about what it means to matter to a loved one. Not in the grand sense of a legacy he'll leave or the impact he'll have, but in the intimate way that one life shapes another. He has always believed his role as a father is to prepare his son for the world, but he now shifts to preparing his son for a world without him.

After Derek and I have many sessions supporting the facing of his own reality, Derek is able to speak more honestly about his fear. Not just of death but of leaving those he loves more than life behind. We discuss how he will always be carried by those he loves, even if he isn't physically present. Mattering to others isn't something that's undone by death.

Although his days aren't easier, he does have more clarity, sinking into each moment, reveling in his son's laughter and the glow of his wife's beauty. *It's time,* he thinks. Caught off guard at how calm he is, he sits next to his son and gently tells him the news. Tears flowing, Derek embraces it all, allowing his son to share in his father's anger while also being a compassionate witness to his own sadness and fear.

His son is willing to take the risk of knowing his father—a risk he is thankful for taking. Over the next two months, they walk in the backyard, collecting stones and leaves, while his son asks questions about Derek's own childhood: "Did you ever get in really big trouble? Did you always want to have kids?" Eventually, he asks, "Are you afraid to die?"

One day, seemingly out of the blue, Derek's son tells him, "You'll always be with me. I'll still have talks with you." And in that moment, Derek feels relief: *He's going to be okay.* He'll feel pain and loss and grief, but Derek feels certain that his son is going to be okay.

Derek died two months later, leaving his son with connection and more peace than he would have had had Derek continued to hide. By allowing himself to bear witness to his own suffering, be available and present to his son's, and, most important, bear witness to each other's despair, Derek taught his son an important lesson about what matters most: Mattering isn't about how long we are around; it's about how deeply we love—the imprints we leave on others, the way we show up for them, and the ways we choose to care. The effects of mattering linger in the way we carry on and continue to love.

How to Matter

Existential mattering is key for all of us. What do we tell ourselves about how much we are valued by those around us and how much we mean to others? Whether it's seeing friends and family, giving toasts at graduations or birthdays, or having neighbors set up a meal plan after the birth of a child, as humans, we need to believe that we matter to others.

Unfortunately, too often existential mattering is in short supply. With more and more focus on ourselves, consumed with our own thoughts, emotions, agendas, or priorities, we have little left over to recognize and help others feel that they matter. But we can do this for each other in small ways throughout the day—grabbing tea for a colleague before a meeting or buying a souvenir for a friend while on vacation.

We don't always think about how we're connecting to ourselves when we're talking about relationships. Most of the relationship advice I see focuses on ways of communicating or guided behavioral exercises to foster a sense of connection. When I look at friends who are in mutually respectful relationships where both feel truly partnered, supported, and adored—even in the struggles of early family life, with working parents and young kids—they don't have scripts of communication and they don't engage in stereotyped exercises.

Listening well isn't just summarizing or paraphrasing. It's bearing witness to someone's suffering to know they're not alone. The hard part is that hearing others' suffering can naturally create our own. As words reach us, we turn our attention inward. Inadvertently, we avoid the conversation or downplay the sufferer's pain. Yet doing so can silence the sufferer, making them feel more apprehensive and alone.

I've found that the success of one's ability to connect with others depends on our ability to connect to our own suffering. The more we understand our own inner experiences, the better we can recognize and respond to the struggles of others. When we do, the benefits aren't just emotional.

Having a reliable listener can actually help stave off cognitive decline—even if one has a neuropathological disease like dementia. In a multisite study, neurologist Joel Salinas and colleagues used one of the longest-running community-based cohorts in the United States (the Framingham Heart Study) to determine how having someone available to talk to when needed affects the brain. Researchers examined records of 2,171 participants who self-reported on the availability of five forms of social interactions—listening, good advice, love and affection, having sufficient contact with close ones, and emotional support. Researchers then looked at participants' brain MRIs, as lower brain volumes tend to be associated with lower cognitive functioning.

They found that having someone who will listen to you during a time of need can actually slow down cognitive aging and even prevent the development of symptoms of dementia. Moreover, for every unit of brain volume decline, middle-aged adults in their forties and fifties who had low listener availability had a cognitive age that was four years *older* than those who had someone to talk to.

All of which is to say that having someone listen to you is good for your brain health. But listening is both a gift to give and to keep at the same time. Deep listening can also rewire the listener's brain, strengthening attention, emotion regulation, and the neural circuitry for empathy. It's a feedback loop that leaves everyone a little wiser, calmer, and more human.

We've all listened to loved ones suffering through the more common difficulties: affairs, breakups, illnesses, and loss. How we engage with their suffering depends on our ability to do a deep dive to see and share the struggle. The process of how we engage with our and another's suffering can allow us to become more wise—more free. Bearing witness and listening to another's struggles won't necessarily take away their pain, but it tells your beloved that they won't have to hold it alone. Showing up means training ourselves to approach, even when our instincts tell us to withdraw.

Action Tools for Mattering

A. Mattering and Meaning

1. Redefine success by how deeply you affect, not achieve. Purpose isn't something stumbled upon in a single moment of clarity but rather an intricate web of relationships and actions that pull you through life's turbulence. When you feel you don't matter, your brain interprets it as a survival threat. Was there a time this week when someone made you feel significant? How did that feel?

2. Mattering inventory. When we matter, we thrive, and when we thrive, we can give more of ourselves. At what times have you mattered to someone? What are the situations and groups in which you feel you matter?

3. Identify the birds left out of your flock. While we tend to be drawn toward those who are similar to us, we may be excluding others who may actually help us grow. Our brains are wired to trust similarity and reject perceived threat, as we avoid what reminds us of our own vulnerabilities. Embracing our own vulnerabilities helps equip us for the relational ups and downs to come. Identify someone you tend to judge quickly and ask yourself what in them reflects a fear you have. Is there a community or group you could join in which you aren't part of the majority or the expert?

B. Improve Your Social Fitness

4. Prioritize emotional presence over social performance. Social fitness is about being safe to connect with, not just likable— one can be both socially popular and emotionally unfit. How often do you interrupt or pivot conversations back to yourself? Do one daily thing that's connective (e.g., reaching out to someone to check in on how they're doing, not only to share news or vent). What's one thing you'd like to improve about your relational health right now?

5. Relationships as mirrors. Most of our relationships, especially intimate ones, serve as mirrors to reflect parts of ourselves we admire or despise. When you look at your relationships, what do you see about yourself? What do you tell yourself about how much you are valued by those around you and how much you mean to others?

C. Bear Witness to Suffering

6. Build the emotional muscle to stay with discomfort. Most people retreat from others' pain out of discomfort and confusion about how to respond. While being present can make you feel powerless, it's one of the most powerful acts you can offer. The next time someone shares an emotionally heavy or distressing moment, count to ten before speaking and challenge yourself to be present with them—what emotions are coming up? Practice being present and bearing witness to another's suffering. Move beyond emotional listening toward moral witnessing.

7. Connect to your own experience of suffering. It is very hard to connect outward if you are disconnected inward. The depth of your connection with others is limited by your connection to yourself. Check in with yourself through meditation or mindfulness and observe how you're feeling and what you need. Before helping someone, ask yourself if you are trying to fix them to avoid fixing something within yourself.

10

Rethinking
Resilience

I've long felt unsettled by the word *resilience*, which is usually seen as the ability to bounce back after encountering difficulties. If resilience is bouncing back, what are people bouncing back to? The idea of reentering a safe world provides the allure of problems coming to an end and life getting better. But shiny new jobs, travel, and all external distractions eventually dull, leaving people disappointed when old patterns and feelings resurface. We all have this narrative of "If I had this, then I'd be healed." But then we realize it's just not like that. Instability is an equalizer.

There's a prevailing notion that dangers are rare; that if you've experienced anguish, you need to be resilient—get up, barrel through, and keep moving. Fix-it solutions, such as positive thinking, grit, and attending to the present, can and do help us all feel a little bit better—in the short term.

In the face of turmoil, we make the cardinal error of focusing on elimination—getting rid of the problem as quickly as possible. This, of course, makes sense if your life is in danger or under threat. But in a world obsessed with silver linings and toxic positivity, we assume that the most resilient people are those who are able to barrel through major disruptions relatively unaffected—and with a smile.

But what I've learned from my work is that there is no gritting and barreling. If we try to squash the adversity each time it arises, we lose the opportunity to build skills that can prepare us for the next go-round. And doing so actually keeps us suffering over time.

In a world with assured uncertainties, I believe there is a more useful definition of *resilience*: the ability to embrace instability by connecting deeply within and then connecting with a shared sense of humanity. Embracing instability is the bedrock of resilience. Instead of seeing adversity as something to fix, my approach is to validate how adversity is a part of human existence—a truth that will never go away.

Instability is the default, and if we can come to understand and internalize that reality—even before we experience true trauma—we can find the beauty and peace in it and weather the storms when they come. The three friends of winter are our natural instincts that we can tap into to help embrace the unavoidable struggles to come. They help us use resilience as a form of resistance to protect what is soft and sacred, even in harsh terrain. We heal not from sprinting through the instability but from learning how to be human inside it.

Falling with Others

Resilience is often viewed as an individual act. We picture grit, lone-wolf strength, or emotionless perseverance as we summon inner strength and push forward. Turmoil, adversity, and fright all weigh us down, blocking our progress forward. We lose the ability to relate to others as we fall deeper and deeper into isolation. Adversities don't happen only alongside us—they actually *become* us.

Failing to attune to friends and family, we leave them alone, unsure of how to respond to their struggles, or we hide in our own, not wanting to burden others. But what so many definitions of resilience miss is that it's not a solo achievement; it's a relational experience.

We don't heal by ourselves but in the in-between—when someone's willing to sit with us in the hard space where pain is met before being solved. Being relationally resilient invites someone in, even when we feel like a mess.

This is one of the benefits of longer-term psychotherapy—as you allow your pain and longing to surface in the room, something shifts. Shame dissipates as you learn to embrace and, sometimes, even feel pride in the events in the past you were embarrassed about. Vulnerability doesn't stay confined to sessions but can ripple outward, softening the way you show up in the rest of your life too, giving you more confidence. We rise when others stay with us in the fall.

Whatever the threats to our stability—from within or without— how we share ourselves with others is key. Through deep connection with ourselves, we can open to humanity at large and move toward socially responsive engagement to influence the shaping of a world in which we want to live. We may believe we have nothing in common with those who have suffered the most until we bear witness and realize our universal human experiences. Linking collective responsibility to the individual—this is the challenge of our times.

Systems Failure

Real resilience isn't a trait—it's a story. In my early years working as a child psychiatrist and medical director of a foster-care clinic in the Bay Area, I often came across this term, resilience. Caring for children navigating the wreckage of disrupted attachments, multiple placements, and the heartbreak of being moved from home to home, sometimes with only minutes' notice, I often heard these children labeled *resilient*. The word was meant to praise—a nod to their intelligence, adaptability, and courage.

Yet I found it troubling. I had questions about the way the word was used: *Who gets to define* resilience? *Who benefits from naming it?* Too often, the term was used by those far removed from the daily lives of these children—professionals like me, administrators, and policymakers. In the naming was a quiet distancing, admiring these children's strengths without interrogating the systems that required such strength. It's much easier to call a child resilient than to ask, *Why did this child have to be so strong in the first place?*

Resilience, as we often speak of it, risks glorifying survival in environments that should never have required it, turning adaptation into isolation and endurance into silence. For so many of the people that I work with, adversity isn't random; it's patterned and systematized in a deeply unequal distribution of safety, stability, and care.

And yet the burden to overcome these conditions falls on the individual. This is the quiet cruelty of how we often frame resilience—as a way to celebrate someone's ability to endure while doing little to change what they are enduring. Essentially, we're saying: *We couldn't fix the system, so you need to survive it.* While this book focuses on the journey of seeing pain close up, my daily work is focused in equal parts on understanding it and changing the structures that produce it.

So what is resilience, really? Resilience isn't resignation. True resilience doesn't ask us to accept the unacceptable but to respond to adversity by refusing to lose ourselves in the process. To me, it's not about submission or quietly surviving what was never acceptable.

Resilience is rooted in the ability to see clearly, feel deeply, prepare, adapt, connect, and resist becoming numb by embracing the instabilities that come our way and reclaiming our humanity. But it's also about building systems that don't demand resilience. While admirable, resilience is often the result of a system that has failed. The real work isn't only in helping people bounce back individually but in creating structures that don't push them down. If we want to honor resilience, we have to start by asking why it is needed at all.

I want to reimagine resilience not as armor but as aliveness. It's not a destination but a bridge toward justice, belonging, and safety. We need to move beyond resilience as a heroic act of solitude toward a deeply human response to suffering that invites healing, intimacy, and the possibility of change.

Embracing instability is a skill to be developed, like playing basketball or cooking. The irony is, most schools and workplaces don't teach any of this—how to sit inside uncertainty, how to lean on each other, and how to question the systems we're navigating. Instead, we rely on individuals stumbling alone through life to figure it out without guidance. But it doesn't have to be this way. We aren't meant to do this alone.

The good news is this is entirely possible. Current research shows that resilience is both time- and context-dependent. It's not a trait; it's a dynamic process. We aren't born either resilient or not, a fact that should give us all hope. We can learn to be resilient at any age and no matter our circumstance. It doesn't take a revolution, just reorientation, starting with small choices, thoughtful environments, and the intention to do things differently.

Tree-Schoolers

My children were in an all-weather, all-outdoor preschool, with a forty-acre sanctuary as their classroom. In the winter, these tree-schoolers double-layered under their snow pants, sat on "nature cookies" (tree stumps) during snack time, and examined decaying deer bones as part of their curriculum.

As my children's favorite teacher, Amelia, said, "There are three basic mechanisms of survival when the temperatures drop: adaptation, hibernation, and migration." It turns out that nature preschool teaches us all we need to know about resilience: To internalize the harshness of winter, we should prepare, adapt, and share.

These tree-schoolers embrace the harshness of winter with wonder. Heavy, wet snow and sleet were seen as a common aspect of nature to respect and embrace, not shun. By visiting familiar spots as the weather changed, the kids were given the opportunity to embrace changes with curiosity.

Even hidden narratives were explored in nature school, as confusion about the daily observations of missing pumpkins were explored with a "trap cam." Setting up a night-vision camera, teachers were able to catch images of nocturnal foxes and raccoons taking turns munching on the pumpkin seeds the class left for them.

At pickup, I always anticipated a sigh or fatigue from a day of freezing temperatures, but I was often met with "Mommy! We saw footprints on the snow!" The narrative of these children was one of interconnectedness: Nature, life, and our communities are full of wonder, to be respected and cared for. Harsh conditions can be met with joy.

This was embodied in their ritual of "sit spots": five minutes of quiet stillness, actively observing the natural environment. The nature preschool wasn't just play but the early tending of something much deeper: They were growing a garden of resilience, rooted in connection, supported by a structure that allowed for risk, curiosity, and care.

Walking on ice and snow requires energy, focus, concentration, and balance. Heavier clothing feels burdensome. A deliberate change in movements that's different from the automatic rhythms of summer is necessary. When we start out with an intention to embrace instability and shift our narratives and rituals toward a purpose, we may feel unsteady. We don't know how to begin and may look to others for answers. When we direct the search from within, new questions arise: *Does this remind me of a past adversity? How did I get through it? Has my narrative about it changed over time? What rituals helped me? Who supported me? Where can I matter?*

Suffering has a lot to teach us about ourselves and others. It can hurt, but it doesn't have to. Healing isn't about erasing the past or powering through it. Resilience, I believe, is shaped in relationships, meaning, and environments that give us room to fall and be met without shame. This book has been about those personal acts of repair—messy, human, and hard-won. But healing doesn't end at the individual level. It begins there.

We tend to treat resilience as the goal—as if the highest form of growth is the ability to endure. But endurance without reflection can become numbness. I didn't write this book because I've figured it all out—I won't pretend I've mastered resilience. I still break, still question, and still carry more than I let show. But what's changed is how I carry it and who I let carry it with me. I've stopped chasing the illusion of stability. I no longer believe resilience is the destination.

I see it more as a name we give to bringing ourselves alongside the suffering and staying human when the world asks us not to be. The most resilient people I know aren't the ones who survived the hardest times. They're the ones who showed up for themselves and turned their healing into a way forward for others.

ACKNOWLEDGMENTS

Writing a book may be a solitary act, but behind every paragraph stand those whose influence is woven into the work through challenge, through joy, through the moments when the next step feels impossible. This is the rare chance to step back and trace the constellation of people who, knowingly or not, carried me through personally and professionally.

I begin with gratitude for my family. Generations of ancestors whose lives ripple forward through mine, a father whose presence endures beyond his years on this earth, and loved ones across the ocean in Korea who continue to hold a part of me from afar. And my children, for whom this book was ultimately written. Their generosity of spirit, love of learning, and courageous kindness serve as a guiding light in their own right. They may see me as the mother who organizes playdates, throws birthday parties for our pets, and volunteers as the room parent every year. But I also wanted to leave something enduring: lessons gathered from those I've met in far corners of the world, distilled into a compass to carry anywhere.

In the hardest seasons, I've leaned on my mother—needed more in my forties than ever before, who has always shown up and found a way forward when no one else could—and my brother, who has the uncanny habit of appearing during my most difficult seasons to remind me that I'm not alone. Our small family has shown how far love can travel.

I became a psychiatrist to ease suffering—treating healing as an art and a science, advocating for the misunderstood, and shaping systems that amplify human strengths. Bearing witness to another's most unguarded moments is one of life's profound privileges. Everyone I have worked with, in clinic offices, refugee settlements, research interviews, and professional trainings, whether for an hour or over a decade, has offered trust, courage, and unspoken lessons in resilience that no textbook could teach.

The ideas in this book were written in a crucible of lived experience: divorce, a house fire, displacement, and political unrest that upended my work. Life itself became a testing ground for every principle I share here. The "three friends of winter" proved reliable companions, especially when shared with friends whose constancy endured all seasons: Irene Lopez, whose unwavering presence, generous heart, irreverent humor, and unflinching wisdom throughout our fifteen years of sisterhood have kept the breaking point just out of reach. Susan Oviedo Lebowitz, whose care has been an anchor from high school summers to tempered middle-aged winters. Camilla Dorment, whose tenderness reveals its own quiet form of bravery.

The development of this book was sustained by a remarkable publishing team. My astute literary agent, Richard Pine, brought a discerning vision that unearthed truths from me I didn't know were there. His influence—along with editor Shannon Welch, who encouraged me to step more fully into my own story—changed the book's course and my own. Editors Diana Baroni skillfully assembled scattered pieces into coherence, and Donna Loffredo approached the manuscript with acumen and care, engaging in a way that elevated the work while honoring its essence. Copy editor Tracy Roe reviewed with precision and persistence, while US editor Matthew Benjamin and UK editor Olivia Morris offered astute, clarifying reads. The wider Harmony and Penguin Random House teams—spanning production managers, proofreaders, designers, and the many behind-the-scenes hands that guided this book from draft to finished work—carried it with care until it could stand on its own.

The lens through which much of this work was written was sharpened by colleagues devoted to easing human suffering, whether through direct service, policy, programming, advocacy, or research. Clinical teams at Asian Americans for Community Involvement and Northern Virginia Family Services; colleagues Jessie Kendall, Claudia Zaborsky, and Jessa Crisp, whose work confronts human trafficking and upholds the dignity of survivors; mentors William Greenberg, Roberta Apfel, Carl Feinstein, and James Griffith—each recognized a promise in me that was not yet self-evident.

Beyond borders, partnerships with the MHPSS Collaborative of Save the Children Denmark, UNICEF, the International Medical Corps, and countless peers—across roles, agencies, and changing affiliations—have deepened the understanding of healing in complex contexts. Doctoral advisers Joop de Jong, Wietse Tol, and Charlie Kaplan anchored that global perspective with enduring mentorship.

When disaster stripped away belongings and workspace, other communities lifted me: my yoga family—Cheryl Amick, Lee Altobello, Larry Barnett, Stacy Hartranft, Dave Terzian, and the wider community—functioned as my church; my local moms' group and neighborhood book club offered the balm of shared laughter and quiet solidarity; the lady docs group stood as proof of the fierce, sustaining force of women bound by profession and dedication.

Like many mothers, my peace rises and falls with knowing my children are cared for and respected. For those who have loved my children into confidence and kindness, thank you for the comfort you've given us.

Every encounter, whether fleeting or sustained, has left an imprint on this work. My hope is that what began here returns to the world carrying the same quiet resilience, daring connection, and stubborn faith in one another that made it possible.

NOTES

x   displaced Syrian teens: Suzan Song, "Mental Health/Psychosocial and Child Protection Assessment for Syrian Refugee Adolescents in Za'atari Refugee Camp, Jordan," International Medical Corps and United Nations Children's Fund, July 2013, http://reliefweb.int/sites/reliefweb.int/files /resources/IMC%20MHPSS%20and%20CP%20Assessment%20Zaa-tari%20July%202013%20final%20%281%29.pdf.

x   impact of child soldiering: Suzan J. Song and Joop de Jong, "The Role of Silence in Burundian Former Child Soldiers," International Journal for the Advancement of Counselling 36, no. 1 (2014): 84–95; Suzan Song et al., "Children of Former Child Soldiers and Never-Conscripted Civilians: A Preliminary Intergenerational Study in Burundi," Journal of Aggression, Maltreatment, and Trauma 22, no. 7 (2013): 757–72; Suzan Song et al., "Indero: Intergenerational Trauma and Resilience Between Burundian Former Child Soldiers and Their Children," Family Process 53, no. 2 (2014): 239–51.

xi   soldiers as "comfort women": Chunghee Sarah Soh, The Comfort Women: Sexual Violence and Postcolonial Memory in Korea and Japan (University of Chicago Press, 2008).

xii   who doesn't quite fit in: Kristin Long, "Fractured Stories: Self-Experiences of Third Culture Kids," Journal of Infant, Child, and Adolescent Psychotherapy 19, no. 2 (2020): 134–47.

xv   multiple worlds of healing: Suzan J. Song, "An Ethical Approach to Life-Long Learning: Implications for Global Psychiatry," Academic Psychiatry 35, no. 6 (November 2011): 391–96.

xvi   long after the war: Theresa S. Betancourt et al., "Sierra Leone's Former

Child Soldiers: A Follow-Up Study of Psychosocial Adjustment and Community Reintegration," *Child Development* 81, no. 4 (2010): 1077–95.

xvi   In Sierra Leone: Suzan J. Song, Helene van den Brink, and Joop de Jong, "Who Cares for Former Child Soldiers? Mental Health Systems of Care in Sierra Leone," *Community Mental Health Journal* 49, no. 5 (2013): 615–24.

xvi   and Liberia: Suzan J. Song et al., "A Mental Health Needs Assessment of Children and Adolescents in Post-Conflict Liberia: Results from a Quantitative Key-Informant Survey," *International Health* 8, no. 1 (2016): 1–8.

xvi   estimated 250,000 children: "Recruitment of Child Soldiers Is on the Rise, Despite Global Commitments," United Nations Office at Geneva, December 31, 2024, https://www.ungeneva.org/en/news-media/news/2024/12/101829/recruitment-child-soldiers-rise-despite-global-commitments.

xvii vulnerable to coercion: Suzan J. Song and Joop de Jong, "Child Soldiers: Children Associated with Fighting Forces," *Child and Adolescent Psychiatric Clinics of North America* 24, no. 4 (October 2015): 765–75.

xxii *isolation of affect*: George E. Vaillant, *Ego Mechanisms of Defense: A Guide for Clinicians and Researchers*, 2nd ed. (American Psychiatric Association, 1992), 85–102.

xxv   The researchers found: Archy O. de Berker et al., "Computations of Uncertainty Mediate Acute Stress Responses in Humans," *Nature Communications* 7 (March 29, 2016): 10996.

xxvii Identity is shaped *with* others: Susan E. Cross, Pamela L. Bacon, and Michael L. Morris, "The Relational-Interdependent Self-Construal and Relationships," *Journal of Personality and Social Psychology* 78, no. 4 (2000): 791–808.

xxvii loneliness epidemic: Vivek H. Murthy, "Loneliness and Isolation Are an Epidemic, and the U.S. Must Address It," US Department of Health and Human Services, May 2023, https://www.hhs.gov/about/news/2023/05/02/loneliness-isolation-epidemic-us-must-address-it.html.

5   inner dialogue controls: Hubert J. M. Hermans and Giancarlo Dimaggio, "The Dialogical Self: Meaning as Movement," *International Journal for Dialogical Science* 1, no. 1 (2006): 1–28.

9   what they do next: Daniel Kahneman and Amos Tversky, "Prospect Theory: An Analysis of Decision Under Risk," *Econometrica* 47, no. 2 (1979): 263–91.

9   "to change ourselves": Viktor E. Frankl, *Man's Search for Meaning*, trans. Ilse Lasch (Beacon Press, 2006).

10   *through identity scripts*: Kate C. McLean, Monisha Pasupathi, and Moin Syed, "Cognitive Scripts and Narrative Identity Are Shaped by Structures of Power," *Trends in Cognitive Sciences* 27, no. 9 (2023): 805–13.

11   how people became leaders: Herminia Ibarra, *Working Identity: Unconventional Strategies for Reinventing Your Career* (Harvard Business School Press, 2003).

11 now-classic study: Herminia Ibarra, "Provisional Selves: Experimenting with Image and Identity in Professional Adaptation," *Administrative Science Quarterly* 44, no. 4 (1999): 764–91.

11 experimented with new narratives: Herminia Ibarra and Roxana Barbulescu, "Identity as Narrative: A Process Model of Narrative Identity Work in Macro Work Role Transition," *Academy of Management Review* 35, no. 1 (2010): 135–54.

12 the "mimetic mind": Merlin Donald, *Origins of the Modern Mind: Three Stages in the Evolution of Culture and Cognition* (Harvard University Press, 1991).

12 development of alloparenting: Sarah Blaffer Hrdy, *Mother Nature: A History of Mothers, Infants, and Natural Selection* (Pantheon, 1999).

12 fire-making: Richard Wrangham, *Catching Fire: How Cooking Made Us Human* (Basic Books, 2009).

13 "then they changed us": Daniel Dor, *The Instruction of Imagination: Language as a Social Communication Technology* (Oxford University Press, 2015).

13 fill in the blanks: Roy F. Baumeister and Leonard S. Newman, "How Stories Make Sense of Personal Experiences: Motives That Shape Autobiographical Narratives," *Journal of Personality and Social Psychology* 69, no. 3 (1995): 432–44.

16 rebalances the brain: James S. Nairne, Sarah R. Thompson, and Josefa N. S. Pandeirada, "Adaptive Memory: Survival Processing Enhances Retention," *Journal of Experimental Psychology: Learning, Memory, and Cognition* 33, no. 2 (2007): 263–80.

16 *externalization of blame:* June P. Tangney et al., "Shaming, Blaming, and Maiming: Functional Links Among the Moral Emotions, Externalization of Blame, and Aggression," *Journal of Research in Personality* 44, no. 1 (2010): 91–102.

16 cognitive-distortion biases: Aaron T. Beck et al., *Cognitive Therapy of Depression* (Guilford Press, 1979).

17 interrogate them with curiosity: Daniel M. Wegner, "Ironic Processes of Mental Control," *Psychological Review* 101, no. 1 (1994): 34–52.

18 more balanced way: M. S. H. Huang et al., "Cognitive Reappraisal and Self-Compassion as Emotion Regulation Strategies for Parents During COVID-19: An Online Randomized Controlled Trial," *Frontiers in Psychology* 12 (2021): 688011.

18 three main forces: Silvan S. Tomkins, *Affect Imagery Consciousness*, vols. 1–4 (Springer, 1962–1992).

18 Of these, affects: Tomkins, *Affect Imagery Consciousness*, vol. 2.

21 *affect phobia:* Leigh McCullough et al., *Treating Affect Phobia: A Manual for Short-Term Dynamic Psychotherapy* (Guilford Press, 2003).

22 provide you with temporary relief: Steven C. Hayes, Kirk D. Strosahl, and Kelly G. Wilson, *Acceptance and Commitment Therapy: An Experiential Approach to Behavior Change* (Guilford Press, 1999).

34   more like a movie editor: Daniel L. Schacter, *The Seven Sins of Memory: How the Mind Forgets and Remembers* (Houghton Mifflin, 2001), 16.

34   playing a tennis match: Eric R. Kandel, James H. Schwartz, and Thomas M. Jessell, *Principles of Neural Science,* 4th ed. (McGraw Hill, 2000).

36   survival mechanism: Kasia Kozlowska et al., "Fear and the Defense Cascade: Clinical Implications and Management," *Harvard Review of Psychiatry* 23, no. 4 (2015): 263–87.

37   *Dissociative amnesia:* Angelica Staniloiu and Hans J. Markowitsch, "Dissociative Amnesia," *The Lancet Psychiatry* 1, no. 3 (2014): 226–41.

37   burden of proof: Suzan J. Song, "Mental Health of Unaccompanied Children: Effects of U.S. Immigration Policies," *British Journal of Psychiatry Open* 7, no. 6 (2021): e200.

38   "sins of memory": Schacter, *The Seven Sins of Memory,* 51–74.

39   "remembering self": Daniel Kahneman, *Thinking, Fast and Slow* (Farrar, Straus and Giroux, 2011).

40   trauma can interfere: Martin H. Teicher et al., "Developmental Neurobiology of Childhood Stress and Trauma," *Psychiatric Clinics of North America* 25, no. 2 (2002): 397–426.

40   "collaborative remembering": William Hirst and Gerald Echterhoff, "Remembering in Conversations: The Social Sharing and Reshaping of Memories," *Annual Review of Psychology* 63 (2012): 55–79.

41   prevent memory distortions: Heather Bacon, Sarah L. Goodwin, and Martine B. Powell, "Preserving the Past: An Early Interview Improves Delayed Event Memory in Children with Intellectual Disabilities," *Memory* 24, no. 5 (2016): 628–35.

42   one in four college women: Cantor, D., Fisher, B., Chibnall, S., Harps, S., Townsend, R., Thomas, G., Lee, H., Kranz, V., Herbison, R., & Madden, K. (2019). Report on the AAU Climate Survey on Sexual Assault and Sexual Misconduct. Association of American Universities.

44   *post-traumatic stress disorder* (PTSD): "Post-Traumatic Stress Disorder (PTSD)," National Institute of Mental Health, last modified December 2024, https://www.nimh.nih.gov/health/topics/post-traumatic-stress-disorder-ptsd.

48   *repetition compulsion:* Sanford Gifford, "The Repetition Compulsion," *Journal of the American Psychoanalytic Association* 12, no. 3 (1964): 473–85.

49   embedded deep in the brain: Bruce S. McEwen, *The End of Stress as We Know It: How Neuroscience and Brain Plasticity Can Transform Your Life* (Dana Press, 2007).

53   rats to navigate: Kyle S. Smith et al., "Reversible Online Control of Habitual Behavior by Optogenetic Manipulation of Prefrontal Cortex," *Proceedings of the National Academy of Sciences* 110, no. 4 (January 29, 2013): 1654–59.

54   Self-reflection with an engaged: Carl R. Rogers, *On Becoming a Person: A Therapist's View of Psychotherapy* (Boston: Houghton Mifflin, 1961).

60 visualizing an outcome: Linda Solbrig et al., "Functional Imagery Training Versus Motivational Interviewing for Weight Loss: A Randomised Controlled Trial of Brief Individual Interventions for Overweight and Obesity," *International Journal of Obesity* 43, no. 4 (2019): 883–94.

69 separation, liminality, and reintegration: Arnold van Gennep, *The Rites of Passage,* trans. Monika B. Vizedom and Gabrielle L. Caffee (University of Chicago Press, 1960).

71 jeopardize your sense of security: Stevan E. Hobfoll, "Conservation of Resources: A New Attempt at Conceptualizing Stress," *American Psychologist* 44, no. 3 (1989): 516–17.

72 perform better: D. J. Foster et al., "The Effect of Removing Superstitious Behavior and Introducing a Pre-Performance Routine on Basketball Free-Throw Performance," *Journal of Applied Sport Psychology* 18, no. 2 (2006): 145–55.

72 improve social bonding: Sarah J. Charles et al., "United on Sunday: The Effects of Secular Rituals on Social Bonding and Affect," *PLOS One* 16, no. 1 (2021): e0242546.

72 define a ritual: Alison W. Brooks et al., "Don't Stop Believing: Rituals Improve Performance by Decreasing Anxiety," *Organizational Behavior and Human Decision Processes* 137 (2016): 71–85.

73 communities with robust shared rituals: Roshan Bhakta Bhandari et al., "Building a Disaster-Resilient Community Through Ritual-Based Social Capital: A Brief Analysis of Findings from the Case Study of Kishiwada," *Disaster Prevention Research Institute Annuals* 53 (2010): 16–25.

74 fire-walking ritual: Ronald Fischer et al., "The Fire-Walker's High: Affect and Physiological Responses in an Extreme Collective Ritual," *PLOS One* 9, no. 2 (2014): e88355.

74 *collective effervescence:* Émile Durkheim, *The Elementary Forms of Religious Life,* trans. Karen E. Fields (Free Press, 1995).

75 series of experiments: Michael I. Norton and Francesca Gino, "Rituals Alleviate Grieving for Loved Ones, Lovers, and Lotteries," *Journal of Experimental Psychology: General* 143, no. 1 (2014): 266–72.

76 symbolic behaviors honor: Corina Sas and Alina Coman, "Designing Personal Grief Rituals: An Analysis of Symbolic Objects and Actions," *Death Studies* 40, no. 9 (2016): 558–69.

77 instinctively reach backward: Constantine Sedikides et al., "Nostalgia: Past, Present, and Future," *Current Directions in Psychological Science* 17, no. 5 (2008): 304–7.

78 faced with psychological threats: Xinyue Zhou et al., "Counteracting Loneliness: On the Restorative Function of Nostalgia," *Psychological Science* 19, no. 10 (October 2008): 1023–29.

78 *positivity bias:* Margaret W. Matlin and David Stang, "The Pollyanna Hypothesis," *Journal of Personality and Social Psychology* 36, no. 8 (1978): 845–55.

79   sink into their regrets: David B. Newman et al., "Nostalgia and Well-Being in Daily Life: An Ecological Validity Perspective," *Journal of Personality and Social Psychology* 118, no. 2 (2019): 325–47.

81   promotes cognitive closure: David A. Sbarra, Hillary L. Smith, and Matthias R. Mehl, "Tell Me a Story: The Creation of Narrative as a Mechanism for Emotional Recovery Following Divorce," *Journal of Social and Clinical Psychology* 36, no. 5 (2017): 359–85.

81   fully engage in emotional integration: Benjamin J. Roth et al., "Benefits of Emotional Integration and Costs of Emotional Distancing: Investigating Expressive Writing About Stress," *Journal of Personality* (2017).

81   task reinforces behavioral commitment: Daniel Ekers et al., "Behavioural Activation for Depression: An Update of Meta-Analysis of Effectiveness and Sub-Group Analysis," *PLOS One* 9, no. 6 (2014): e100100.

83   same neural circuits: Naomi I. Eisenberger and Matthew D. Lieberman, "Why Rejection Hurts: A Common Neural Alarm System for Physical and Social Pain," *Trends in Cognitive Sciences* 8, no. 7 (2004): 294–300.

90   *compounded grief*: Therese A. Rando, *Treatment of Complicated Mourning* (Research Press, 1993).

91   *ambiguous loss*: Pauline Boss, "Ambiguous Loss: Working with Families of the Missing," *Family Process* 41, no. 1 (2002): 14–17.

94   Studies show: Dan W. Grupe and Jack B. Nitschke, "Uncertainty and Anticipation in Anxiety: An Integrated Neurobiological and Psychological Perspective," *Nature Reviews Neuroscience* 14, no. 7 (2013): 488–501.

94   immobilizing them: Boss, "Ambiguous Loss."

95   neurobiological response: Stephen W. Porges, "The Polyvagal Theory: Neurophysiological Foundations of Emotions, Attachment, Communication, and Self-Regulation," *Neuropsychology Review* 17, no. 2 (2007): 111–45.

96   changing one's perspective: Ellen A. Skinner et al., "Searching for the Structure of Coping: A Review and Critique of Category Systems for Classifying Ways of Coping," *Psychological Bulletin* 129, no. 2 (2003): 216–69.

97   denial aren't helpful: Charles S. Carver, Michael F. Scheier, and Jagdish K. Weintraub, "Assessing Coping Strategies: A Theoretically Based Approach," *Journal of Personality and Social Psychology* 56, no. 2 (1989): 267–83.

97   distractions can be: Susan Nolen-Hoeksema and Blair E. Davis, "The Role of Rumination and Distraction in the Coping Process," *Journal of Personality and Social Psychology* 64, no. 6 (1993): 952–61.

97   Distraction and avoidance: Christian E. Waugh, Elaine Z. Shing, and R. Michael Furr, "Not All Disengagement Coping Strategies Are Created Equal: Positive Distraction, but Not Avoidance, Can Be an Adaptive Coping Strategy for Chronic Life Stressors," *Anxiety, Stress, and Coping* 33, no. 5 (2020): 511–29.

97   *positive distractions:* Susan Folkman and Judith Tedlie Moskowitz, "Positive

Affect and the Other Side of Coping," *American Psychologist* 55, no. 6 (2000): 647–54.

98 problems more effectively: Ellen A. Skinner et al., "Searching for the Structure of Coping: A Review and Critique of Category Systems for Classifying Ways of Coping," *Psychological Bulletin* 129, no. 2 (2003): 216–69.

101 full-scale offensive: "Russia's 'Unlawful' Attacks on Civilian Areas in Ukraine," Human Rights Watch, March 2022.

101 enforced disappearances: United Nations Human Rights Monitoring Mission in Ukraine, "Ukraine: Human Rights Situation Remains Bleak Three Years After Russia's Full-Scale Armed Attack," United Nations, March 2025.

101 19,500 children: "Deportation, Treatment of Ukraine's Children by Russian Federation Take Centre Stage by Many Delegates at Security Council Briefing," press release SC/15395, United Nations Security Council, August 24, 2023.

101 children forcibly removed: James Glanz et al., "Ukraine War Has Taken a Devastating Toll on Children," *New York Times*, December 26, 2023.

102 doesn't heal wounds: Daniel J. Siegel, *The Developing Mind: How Relationships and the Brain Interact to Shape Who We Are*, 2nd ed. (Guilford Press, 2012).

103 *hope modules*: James L. Griffith, "Hope Modules: Brief Psychotherapeutic Interventions to Counter Demoralization from Daily Stressors of Chronic Illness," *Academic Psychiatry* 42, no. 1 (2018): 135–45.

103 something you do: Kaethe Weingarten, "Reasonable Hope: Construct, Clinical Applications, and Supports," *Family Process* 49, no. 1 (2010): 5–25.

104 *shift-and-persist problem-solving*: Edith Chen and Gregory E. Miller, " 'Shift-and-Persist' Strategies: Why Being Low in Socioeconomic Status Isn't Always Bad for Health," *Perspectives on Psychological Science* 7, no. 2 (2012): 135–58.

105 social-cognition system: Mina Cikara and Susan T. Fiske, "Social Neuroscience of Intergroup Relations: An Integrative Review," *Trends in Cognitive Sciences* 16, no. 2 (2012): 119–27.

106 suicidal thoughts: Thomas E. Joiner, *Why People Die by Suicide* (Harvard University Press, 2005).

111 impacts of Hurricane Katrina: Sandro Galea et al., "Exposure to Hurricane-Related Stressors and Mental Illness After Hurricane Katrina," *JAMA Psychiatry* 64, no. 12 (2007): 1427–34.

114 neurobiology to integrate: Daniel J. Siegel, *Mindsight: The New Science of Personal Transformation* (Bantam Books, 2010).

115 *MWE*: Siegel, *The Developing Mind*.

117 *ritual of integration*: Roy A. Rappaport, *Ritual and Religion in the Making of Humanity* (Cambridge University Press, 1999).

117 cultural heritage: Moin Syed and Adriana Umaña-Taylor, "The Role of

Family Cultural Socialization in Predicting Psychological Functioning Among First-Generation College Students," *Cultural Diversity and Ethnic Minority Psychology* 21, no. 3 (2015): 427–35.

119   girls were also used: Dyan Mazurana and Khristopher Carlson, "From Combat to Community: Girls in Northern Uganda's War," *International Security* 38, no. 1 (2013): 89–113.

121   sense of yourself: Victor W. Turner, *The Ritual Process: Structure and Anti-Structure* (Aldine, 1969).

130   why it matters: David Brooks, *The Second Mountain: The Quest for a Moral Life* (Random House, 2019).

130   meaningful existence: Vlad Costin and Vivian L. Vignoles, "Meaning Is About Mattering: Evaluating Coherence, Purpose, and Existential Mattering as Precursors of Meaning in Life Judgments," *Journal of Personality and Social Psychology* 118, no. 4 (2020): 864–84.

134   defines *purpose*: Martin Pinquart, "Creating a Purpose in Life: A Meta-Analysis," *Ageing International* 45, no. 2 (2020): 107–23.

134   sense of coherence: Aaron Antonovsky, "The Structure and Properties of the Sense of Coherence Scale," *Social Science and Medicine* 36, no. 6 (1993): 725–33.

135   are constantly evolving: Brent W. Roberts and Daniel Mroczek, "Personality Trait Change in Adulthood," *Current Directions in Psychological Science* 17, no. 1 (2008): 31–35.

135   identity is a performance: Erving Goffman, *The Presentation of Self in Everyday Life* (Doubleday, 1959).

139   learned survival: Kenji Yoshino, *Covering: The Hidden Assault on Our Civil Rights* (Random House, 2006).

139   hide core parts: Diane M. Quinn and Rachel K. Chaudoir, "Living with a Concealable Stigmatized Identity: The Impact of Anticipated Stigma, Centrality, Salience, and Cultural Stigma on Psychological Distress and Health," *Journal of Personality and Social Psychology* 97, no. 4 (2009): 634–51.

142   country teetered on the brink: "Cameroon: Crackdown on Protests in February 2008," Human Rights Watch, March 2008.

144   heal through relationships: James A. Coan and John J. B. Allen, "Social Regulation of Emotion," in *Handbook of Emotion Regulation*, ed. James J. Gross (Guilford Press, 2007), 321–36.

144   are born depending: John Bowlby, *Attachment and Loss*, vol. 1 (Basic Books, 1969).

147   vividly imagine: Kennon M. Sheldon and Sonja Lyubomirsky, "How to Increase and Sustain Positive Emotion: The Effects of Expressing Gratitude and Visualizing Best Possible Selves," *Journal of Positive Psychology* 1, no. 2 (2006): 73–82.

147   intention into your subconscious: James R. Doty, *Manifest: How Gratitude Can Grow Your Brain and Heal Your Heart* (Avery, 2021).

153   corrective experiences: Franz Alexander and Thomas M. French, *Psychoanalytic Therapy: Principles and Application* (University of Nebraska Press, 1946).

154   effects of past hurts: Jeremy D. Safran and Zvi Eisler, "Corrective Emotional Experience," in *Encyclopedia of Psychotherapy*, eds. Michel Hersen and William Sledge (Academic Press, 2002), 509–13.

154   that parents' struggles: Marinus H. van Ijzendoorn, "Intergenerational Transmission of Parenting: A Review of Studies in Nonclinical Populations," *Developmental Review* 15, no. 2 (1995): 199–214.

154   long covered: Diana Fosha, *The Transforming Power of Affect: A Model for Accelerated Change* (Basic Books, 2000).

155   essence of our ancestors: Thich Nhat Hanh, *No Death, No Fear: Comforting Wisdom for Life* (Riverhead Books, 2002).

155   past adversities: Vincent J. Felitti et al., "Relationship of Childhood Abuse and Household Dysfunction to Many of the Leading Causes of Death in Adults: The Adverse Childhood Experiences (ACE) Study," *American Journal of Preventive Medicine* 14, no. 4 (1998): 245–58.

155   *intergenerational trauma:* Yael Danieli, *International Handbook of Multigenerational Legacies of Trauma* (Plenum Press, 1998).

156   food shortage: Tessa J. Roseboom et al., "Effects of Prenatal Exposure to the Dutch Famine on Adult Disease in Later Life: An Overview," *Molecular and Cellular Endocrinology* 185, nos. 1–2 (2001): 93–98.

156   passed down for generations: Natan P. F. Kellermann, "Transmission of Holocaust Trauma—An Integrative View," *Psychiatry: Interpersonal and Biological Processes* 64, no. 3 (2001): 256–67.

162   biological mechanisms: Rachel Yehuda and Amy Lehrner, "Intergenerational Transmission of Trauma Effects: Putative Role of Epigenetic Mechanisms," *World Psychiatry* 17, no. 3 (2018): 243–57.

162   trauma alters stress hormones: Rachel Yehuda and Linda M. Bierer, "Transgenerational Transmission of Cortisol and PTSD Risk," *Progress in Brain Research* 167 (2008): 121–35.

163   developing PTSD themselves: Carla Kmett Danielson, Benjamin L. Hankin, and Lisa S. Badanes, "Youth Offspring of Mothers with Posttraumatic Stress Disorder Have Altered Stress Reactivity in Response to a Laboratory Stressor," *Psychoneuroendocrinology* 53 (March 2015): 170–78.

163   known as epigenetics: Michael J. Meaney, "Epigenetics and the Biological Definition of Gene × Environment Interactions," *Child Development* 81, no. 1 (2010): 41–79.

164   *screen memories:* Lucy LaFarge, "The Screen Memory and the Act of Remembering," *International Journal of Psychoanalysis* 93, no. 5 (2012): 1085–104.

165   "every nursery there are ghosts": Selma Fraiberg, Adele Adelson, and Vivian Shapiro, "Ghosts in the Nursery: A Psychoanalytic Approach to the Problems of Impaired Infant-Mother Relationships," *Journal of the American Academy of Child Psychiatry* 6, no. 3 (1967): 387–421.

166   adverse childhood experience: Felitti et al., "Relationship of Childhood Abuse."

167   shapes a person's identity: Bessel A. van der Kolk, *The Body Keeps the Score: Brain, Mind, and Body in the Healing of Trauma* (Viking, 2014).

168   seen hard knocks: Robert D. Schweitzer, Philip Melotte, and Modupe Taiwo, "Early Trauma and Associations with Altruistic Attitudes and Behaviours Among Young Adults," *Child Abuse and Neglect* 122 (2021): 105336.

169   protective factors: Alexandra Crandall et al., "Adverse Childhood Experiences and Counter-ACEs: How Positive and Negative Childhood Experiences Influence Adult Health," *Child Abuse and Neglect* 96 (2019): 104089.

173   crimes against humanity: " 'We Will Erase You From This Land': Crimes Against Humanity and Ethnic Cleansing in Ethiopia's Western Tigray Zone," Amnesty International and Human Rights Watch, April 2022.

173   Villages were razed: "World Report 2022: Ethiopia," Human Rights Watch, 2022.

175   something larger than yourself: Crystal L. Park and Suzanne C. Folkman, "Meaning in the Context of Stress and Coping," *Review of General Psychology* 1, no. 2 (1997): 115–44.

175   their bodies respond: Carol D. Ryff and Burton H. Singer, "Know Thyself and Become What You Are: A Eudaimonic Approach to Psychological Well-Being," *Journal of Happiness Studies* 9, no. 1 (2008): 13–39.

177   after social destruction: "Aftershocks: Women Speak Out Against Sexual Violence in Haiti's Camps," Amnesty International, January 2011.

178   humanitarian parole: Victor Carrion et al., "Building an Effective Medicolegal Intervention Model After the Earthquake in Haiti," *Journal of Child and Adolescent Psychiatry* 29 no. 3 (2012): 61–66.

179   deeper social networks: Maryam Bakhshandeh Bavarsad and Christine Stephens, "Social Network Type Contributes to Purpose in Life Among Older People, Mediated by Social Support," *European Journal of Ageing* 21, no. 1 (January 2024): 5.

179   foundation of being needed: Jan Tønnesvang, "Meaning and Psychological Needs," *Journal of Theoretical and Philosophical Psychology* 45, no. 3 (2025): 316–332.

179   high levels of well-being: Christina D. Falci and Laura A. McClintock Elliott, "Feeling Important, Feeling Well: The Association Between Mattering and Well-Being," *Journal of Happiness Studies* 25, no. 2 (2024): 789–807.

180   Harvard Study of Adult Development: Robert J. Waldinger and Marc S. Schulz, "What's Love Got to Do with It? Social Functioning, Perceived Health, and Daily Happiness in Married Octogenarians," *Psychology and Aging* 27, no. 1 (2012): 42–51.

180   evolved for social connection: Roy F. Baumeister and Mark R. Leary, "The

Need to Belong: Desire for Interpersonal Attachments as a Fundamental Human Motivation," *Psychological Bulletin* 117, no. 3 (1995): 497–529.

181   *mirror-neurons:* Giacomo Rizzolatti and Corrado Sinigaglia, "The Functional Role of the Parieto-Frontal Mirror Circuit: Interpretations and Misinterpretations," *Nature Reviews Neuroscience* 11, no. 4 (2010): 264–74.

181   have all increased: Julianne Holt-Lunstad et al., "Loneliness and Social Isolation as Risk Factors for Mortality: A Meta-Analytic Review," *Perspectives on Psychological Science* 10, no. 2 (2015): 227–37.

182   undeserving of life: Baumeister and Leary, "The Need to Belong."

182   psychological default: Bernadette Park and Nalini Ambady, "Culture and Social Cognition: Evidence from Social Neuroscience," *Annals of the New York Academy of Sciences* 1114, no. 1 (2007): 167–80.

182   our brains operate: Grupe and Nitschke, "Uncertainty and Anticipation in Anxiety."

184   small moments of connection: Harry T. Reis and Shelly L. Gable, "Toward a Positive Psychology of Relationships," in *Flourishing: Positive Psychology and the Life Well-Lived,* eds. Corey L. M. Keyes and Jonathan Haidt (American Psychological Association, 2003), 129–59.

185   a social blanket: Holt-Lunstad et al., "Loneliness and Social Isolation."

185   creating unnecessary pain: Eisenberger and Lieberman, "Why Rejection Hurts."

187   risks of witnessing: Kaethe Weingarten, "Witnessing, Wonder, and Hope," *Family Process* 39, no. 4 (2000): 389–402.

188   face them alone: Ann S. Masten, "Resilience in Children Threatened by Extreme Adversity: Frameworks for Research, Practice, and Translational Synergy," *Development and Psychopathology* 26, no. 4, pt. 2 (2014): 1431–46.

189   *anticipatory grief:* Helen N. Sweeting and Mary L. M. Gilhooly, "Anticipatory Grief: A Review," *Social Science and Medicine* 30, no. 10 (February 1990): 1073–80.

190   Existential mattering: Costin and Vignoles, "Meaning Is About Mattering."

191   multisite study: Joel Salinas et al., "Association of Social Support with Brain Volume and Cognition," *JAMA Network Open* 4, no. 8 (August 2021): e2121122.

INDEX

ABOUT THE AUTHOR

Dr. Suzan Song is a Harvard- and Stanford-trained psychiatrist, humanitarian researcher and adviser. For more than two decades, she has dedicated her work on building resilience in individuals and communities affected by adversity—from everyday struggles to the world's most challenging environments of war and human trafficking. Dr. Song has advised the United Nations and multiple US federal agencies and Ministries of Health, shaping systems of care for children and families in crisis to bridge clinical innovation with systems reform. She has a private practice in Washington, DC, is a professor of psychiatry at George Washington University, and is a sought-after speaker on leadership resilience, systems change, and the science of healing. Her mission is to bridge clinical reality and systemic change, bringing the lessons of human survival into leadership, policy, and programs that can transform lives at scale.